50 EASY AND EFFECTIVE TEACHINGS THAT WILL
TRANSFORM YOU AND THE WORLD AROUND YOU!

Modern Seers Vortexes

A COMPLETE SYSTEM LEADING TO
WISDOM AND SPIRITUAL ADULTHOOD.

A PRACTICAL WAY TO GET
WHAT YOU ***TRULY*** WANT OUT OF LIFE.

Anatole D. Ruslanov, PhD

Modern Seers Publications

Modern Seers Vortexes

ISBN-10: 0615721192   ISBN-13: 978-0615721194

To the Israeli woman, Hungarian man,
American lady, and Norwegian lad
who started me on my journey.

Table of Contents

Table of Contents v

1   The Vortexes: Introduction 1

   1.1   Welcome 2

   1.2   Motivation 4

   1.3   Intention 6

   1.4   The eight sets of Vortexes 8

   1.5   How to engage the Vortexes? 10

2   Universal Vortexes 13

   2.1   Relax, enjoy, and do something useful 14

   2.2   Meditation practice 17

   2.3   Engage teacher: Coaching and mentoring 21

   2.4   Retreats 24

3   Phase I Vortexes: Taste the experience 27

   3.1   Relax, enjoy, and do something useful at Phase I ... 28

   3.2   Insight meditation 30

   3.3   Remember: Better and better! 32

   3.4   Day intending 34

   3.5   Mind influence of others 36

   3.6   Daily deposit 38

   3.7   Uplifting mind-food 40

   3.8   Coaching: Consider 42

   3.9   Retreats at Phase I: Taste 44

4   Phase II Vortexes: Go beyond tasting 47

   4.1   Relax, enjoy, and do something useful at Phase II .. 48

   4.2   Creative visualization meditation 51

   4.3   Avoid upstream thinking 55

4.4	Period intending	....	58
4.5	Pain body	....	60
4.6	Engage Teacher: Experience	....	62
4.7	Balanced life	....	64
4.8	Be yourself	....	66
4.9	Retreats at Phase II: Experience	....	68

5   **Phase III Vortexes: Confirm the experience** 71

5.1	Relax, enjoy, and do something useful at Phase III	.	72
5.2	Nondual meditation	....	74
5.3	Become friendly with the present moment	....	76
5.4	Engage Teacher: Engage	....	78
5.5	Habits	....	80
5.6	Authenticity	....	82
5.7	Madhuvidya	....	84
5.8	Cosmic brotherhood	....	87
5.9	Retreats at Phase III: Validation	....	89

6   **Vortexes for Happy Mind** 91

6.1	Honor your feelings	....	92
6.2	Generosity	....	94
6.3	Admit your mistakes	....	97
6.4	Forgiveness	....	100
6.5	Beauty	....	102
6.6	Healthy food	....	104

7   **Vortexes for Healthy Body** 107

7.1	Honor your body	....	108
7.2	Meditation for healing	....	110
7.3	Drink lots of liquid	....	112
7.4	Good food	....	115
7.5	Exercise	....	118
7.6	Keep clean!	....	120

8   Uplift the World Vortexes 123

   8.1   Respect and appreciate 124

   8.2   Invite up 127

   8.3   Use resources wisely 129

   8.4   Support conscious business 131

   8.5   Engage locally 133

   8.6   Collaborate! 136

9   Vortexes for Inspiring Life 139

   9.1   Action is king 140

   9.2   Perfection 142

   9.3   Focus on positive action 145

   9.4   Question beliefs 147

   9.5   Be here now! 150

Final Thoughts 153

   What's next? 154

   Acknowledgements 155

   About the author 156

   Resources 157

1 The Vortexes: Introduction

Tell me what is it that you plan to do
with your one wild and precious life?
— Mary Oliver

To begin, begin.
— William Wordsworth

1.1 Welcome

If opportunity doesn't knock, build a door.
— Milton Berle

We must welcome the future,
remembering that soon it will be the past;
and we must respect the past, remembering that
it was once all that was humanly possible.
— George Santayana

A vortex is a whirlwind of energy, an irresistible force that draws everything that surrounds it into its current. Modern Seers Vortexes are potent spiritual tools that draw you increasingly toward what you *truly* want. They pull you toward manifesting the desire of your inner being in real life. Reaching out for and engaging the wisdom and passion of your deepest self (your soul) has the side-benefits of living a life of satisfaction, but most importantly it brings the feeling of joy and aliveness to your life.

This book presents a complete system for reconnecting to your deepest being. The Vortexes described in this book — if properly engaged — will consistently bring you into alignment with that Energy which has been called the Great Mystery, Source, Cosmic Consciousness, Supreme Being, etc. The brilliant aliveness of that Energy will shine through you when you become proficient at engaging the Vortexes.

As you "encounter" and engage the Vortexes you will recognize their power in moving you forward. The Vortexes will realign you to focus more on you, the real you, not the constructed you as imposed by your family, culture, your own expectations, and the expectations of others. The Vortexes draw you into your authenticity and call you to meet the real Reality. Meet It directly, walk the walk — meet It raw and unabridged, wild, untidy, exciting, lively!

Read the next few pages first. They explain how to start and what to expect. (Hint: You start by engaging Phase I Vortexes.)

Thank you for picking this book up, from Modern Seers and from the good old Universe as well. Let your life be no less than super amazing, and let the Vortexes be of service in that journey. Live lively!

1.2 Motivation

> The only man I know
> who behaves sensibly is my tailor;
> he takes my measurements anew each time he sees me.
> The rest go on with their old measurements
> and expect me to fit them.
> — George Bernard Shaw

All spiritual traditions aspire to re-connect you to your soul, to your deeper self. But their teachings need to be properly understood and correctly used. Huge problems arise in this endeavor.

Most traditions have their teaching buried in cultural and historical baggage. Currently available spiritual paths definitely contain opportunities for authentic spirituality. On the other hand, all present systems — organized Western religions, New Age approaches, Eastern contemplative traditions, and so on — carry a lot of cultural contamination. This is natural, because these traditions transmit solutions to problems posed by their respective cultures and their respective audiences. Even advanced seekers have problems dealing with such interference — separating culture and history from spiritual instruction and genuine spirituality.

An additional problem is that the spiritual teachings themselves may be outdated. They may have been effective, even state of the art, hundreds of years ago. But, times have changed. New people have come of age, seeking guidance, but the spiritual systems of yesterday have failed to catch up.

Young people today want spiritual practices that are dynamic without being shallow. They want practices that aim at depth without the baggage of outdated traditions. Modern Seers Spiritual Vortexes were designed from the ground up to address these needs of the new generation.

Moreover, the world is moving so fast now that the present cultural traditions have a difficult time keeping up with the speed of new developments. Yesterday's spiritual technology, however state-of-the-art when created, becomes a stagnant belief system laced with dysfunctional or restrictive dogmas. Most of the spiritual traditions of today — however deep — are mired — however subtly — in the old. They do not do a good job addressing new questions, and the needs of today's youth.

Modern Seers spiritual practices, such as these Vortexes and beyond, were designed to be simple, effective, honest, and culturally neutral (universal). They come from 30 years of experience engaging young seekers.

We strongly feel that the Vortexes are a crucial addition to the movement humanity is undergoing in the 21st Century.

1.3 Intention

> Vision without action is merely a dream.
> Action without vision just passes the time.
> Vision with action can change the world.
> — Joel A. Barker

The main intention of Modern Seers Spiritual Vortexes is to be: Simple, Effective, Honest, and Universal.

Let us have a brief look at these four important qualities:

Simple: We humans have a tendency to unnecessarily complicate things, and the spiritual path is no exception. Most traditional systems are collections of complex practices, steeped in long history and deep culture, the spiritual purpose of which has been mostly forgotten.

The Vortexes are simple and approachable practices, stripped down to the necessary essentials. If you truly explore them, you will experience the power of their simplicity. We see no sense for pointless complexity.

Effective: A critically overlooked component of spirituality is effectiveness. We believe that spiritual methods must be evaluated in terms of their effectiveness in reaching their own stated goals. The two questions to ask of any system are: *How does it define success? How well does it achieve success?*

If you practice the Vortexes sincerely and actively you will achieve:

- Less resistance to success
- A more fulfilling life
- More happiness
- More abundance
- Greater health

Honest: The Vortexes do not have ulterior motives behind them, conscious or unconscious. They aim to help you achieve your goals, not to benefit anyone else.

Universal: The Vortexes were designed to work well in all cultures. These practices will benefit you regardless of your history, culture, and religious background.

Today, when so many people are turned off by religion and spirituality, it is good to question why we need a new take on spiritual practices. It is precisely because spiritual practices should be relevant to the people they are intended to serve. The questions spirituality must answer are: *What do we want? How can we get there?* Spiritual practices must answer these questions in the now to be relevant.

1.4 The eight sets of Vortexes

Live your vision and demand your success.
— Steve Maraboli

In order for you to have an idea, a taste of what you are getting yourself into here is the list of all the Vortex sets.

There are eight types of Vortexes, divided into eight groups that address every aspect of your life. Let us take a closer look:

1. Spiritual Vortexes (Phase I) are intended for people who are interested in tasting the experience. This is where you start.

2. Spiritual Vortexes (Phase II) are about letting a solid and serious experience in and achieving some wisdom derived from experience. It is the time to go beyond tasting.

3. Spiritual Vortexes (Phase III) Vortexes are about confirming the experience and waking up to your life and your wisdom, hidden deep in your soul.

4. Universal Vortexes are fundamental teachings that appear at each Phase. These Vortexes are explained separately at the beginning of this book and further described appropriately at each Phase.

5. Happy Mind Vortexes will help keep your mind light and bright — and open to life's new adventures.

6. Healthy Body Vortexes will help keep your physical body healthy and fit for spiritual pursuits.

7. Uplift the World Vortexes are about contributing to the wellbeing of our planet. They are pathways to help people and the world around you to become better.

8. Tips for Inspiring Life are Vortexes that are important advice for spiritual success.

Please read the next segment to learn how to engage the Vortexes. If you are impatient to begin: You should start with practicing Phase I Vortexes, see Page 27.

1.5 How to engage the Vortexes?

> The universe doesn't give you
> what you want in your mind;
> it gives you what you demand with your actions.
> — Steve Maraboli

The Vortexes work well only if you adopt the attitude of action. That is, you must engage the Vortexes for them to be effective. Reading is inspirational but action is about moving forward. Hence, do yourself a favor and start practicing today.

We have grouped the Vortexes into several Phases that we have found to be helpful at particular points of the spiritual journey. The Phases are meant to progressively increase the focus and intensity of your energy. You will do well if you invoke them — incorporate them into your life — in the manner intended. Start with Phase I, continue to Phase II and then Phase III. The Phases are not meant to be restrictive. However, you should let yourself feel the pull towards progression before engaging the "higher" Phase. This will happen in its natural time.

1. Spiritual Vortexes (Phase I: Taste the experience) is where you begin the journey of reinventing yourself. This is a time of refocusing, a soft reinvention, with softness being key. In Phase I, you try things on for size and see how they feel. The important aspects are to give yourself space, let your energy settle, and really come into alignment with yourself.

2. Spiritual Vortexes (Phase II: Go beyond tasting) is where you start to ride the current. Phase II is where the natural momentum really starts picking up. You have become aligned with the more authentic part(s) of yourself. Your energy is becoming more focused. Now that you are more open and clear you become a ready-vessel for wisdom. This might be painful at times as there will still be some holding patterns within that you will try to hold on. But the momentum of practicing the Vortexes will move you beyond these. The key here is to allow the process

to work itself out. And it will! It always does, and it does so more beautifully than you could imagine.

3. Spiritual Vortexes (Phase III: Confirm the experience) is the time to take the reins and become a confident driver. This is where you learn to enjoy the intense beauty of deliberate action and co-creation. At Phase III, you will begin acting from a place of inspiration, not motivation. The difference between these two will truly be understood during this time in the journey. Simply put, motivation is forceful, and inspiration is seamless. The tendency towards the former will become an absurdity, and the tendency towards the latter will flow as natural as sunrise.

There are also two other sets of Vortexes that work in compliment to the primary spiritual Vortexes.

1. The Universal Vortexes are the foundational teachings that are continually applied at all Phases and are explained separately at the beginning of this book and further described appropriately at each Phase.

2. The four sets of Vortexes that apply to the various components of being human. The wisdom found within them will come naturally if you really engage the primary Vortexes, but becoming familiar with them and incorporating them into your life will prove to be fruitful.

i. Happy Mind Vortexes will help keep your mind light and bright — and open to life's new adventures.

ii. Healthy Body Vortexes will help keep your physical body healthy, energized, and fit for spiritual pursuits.

iii. Uplift the World Vortexes are about ways to better people and the world around you.

iv. Tips for Inspiring Life are Vortexes that are important advice for spiritual success.

As you reconnect to your deepest self, a feeling of lightness and lightheartedness comes to you. You begin to shine. And that is why the experiential program that is the companion program to the Vortexes is called Shining Being Training. Your soul begins to shine through — you are happy, playful, and eager for life. If you practice these Vortexes properly you will discover a whole new you and *a real zest to life*.

It is expected that it will take approximately 6 months to ripen the practice of each set of the Vortexes: six months for the Phase I Vortexes, six months for the Phase II Vortexes, and six months for the Phase III Vortexes. Some people may "ripen" their state sooner, in 3 months for example, while others may need up to 12 months or more. Do not practice the Phase II or III Vortexes until you are comfortable and proficient with the Phase I Vortexes. Feel free to look through the further practices to be ready when the time comes.

2 Universal Vortexes

It were better to live one single day in the pursuit of
understanding and meditation,
than to live a hundred years in ignorance and restraint.
— Buddha

The Universal Vortexes are the key themes that appear at all
Phases of Modern Seers Vortexes because they are essential.

2.1 Relax, enjoy, and do something useful

> A good traveler has no fixed plans,
> and no intention of arriving.
> — Lao Tzu

> To have faith is to trust yourself to the water.
> When you swim you don't grab hold of the water,
> because if you do you will sink and drown.
> Instead you relax, and float.
> — Alan Watts

> I have a simple philosophy: Fill what's empty.
> Empty what's full. Scratch where it itches.
> — Alice Roosevelt Longworth

A few years ago a question appeared in my mind while in meditation, "What are my teachings in one sentence?" The answer came quickly: "Relax, enjoy, and do something useful." I like enjoying life, relaxing, eating, going places, and talking to people. While I am laid back, I do not forget about doing something useful. Thus, this Key Vortex came about from my own natural personal life philosophy.

The way I conduct my life is in juxtaposition to the way most people conduct their lives. Most people maintain a pretense of relaxing and enjoying. They also delude themselves about the usefulness of their activities. What most think is useful will not make them happy (or healthy) in the long run. Our world is beset with a perverted sense of responsibility, which replaces real satisfaction and happiness — the two things that make life worthwhile — with ephemeral obligations. This Vortex, at its core, is meant to break the cycle by focusing on what is really important.

Relax: What does it mean to relax? To relax means to let go and let be. Letting go of stiffness in our body, useless concepts or stuck thoughts in the mind, of stuck emotions, of trying to get back at people who hurt us, of guilt about mistakes we have committed. Letting go is about allowing ourselves to start fresh and anew right now.

We could say "meditate always" instead of "relax". In order to truly relax we must relax into the present moment, the point of meditation. If we are not relaxed in the present, our minds are either in the future or in the past — not fully present. Feeling bad about the past or scheming about the future are ways to miss the present.

Enjoy: The present moment is important because the present is all you have — the only space for engaging and enjoying your life. If you focus on the now, you will have a chance to notice gifts that life brings you every moment. Do we need to explain why enjoying your life is important?

Useful: Why did I add "do something useful" to this Vortex? Humans tend to become lazy when relaxation and enjoyment are integrated into their lives. We exist in the world of time-space reality. We need to act and achieve in order to grow, feel good about ourselves, and *earn* our worth to others and ourselves. Graduating from college, getting a job, saving for retirement, and becoming serious about your life and spiritual path are all examples of doing something useful for a better future.

We live in a certain setting, surround ourselves with particular people, and think certain thoughts. The setting, the people, and our thinking define our reality right now. How to escape your present reality? How to find more meaning and joy, away from cooking in your boring and stale soup, away from swimming in a cold and tempestuous river? "Doing something useful" is about finding a peaceful and abundant river, and starting to cook a new, tasty soup.

We create our own reality by methodically advancing toward our desires, in small or big steps. A small step forward would be to begin thinking more productive thoughts. A big accomplishment begins with the first step and proceeds, until done, in small steps. Big or small achievements are always about taking concrete, positive steps to better yourself and your circumstances.

Observe also that the first two practices of this Vortex (relax and enjoy) are prerequisites to the last one (do something useful). To really get going towards what you want, you have to have the first two qualities well developed. If you do not relax, you are not in an allowing state, and it will be very difficult to engage with what you want. You may not even come close to knowing what you want. Take note of where your joy is and follow the path toward your bliss. If you are truly relaxed and truly enjoying, doing something useful will be very easy. It will come out of inspiration rather than motivation.

There is a big difference between these two modes of action. Someone who is motivated is coming from a tense (not relaxed) space. Someone who is inspired is coming from in-spirit-ation. It comes from the Spirit — from your soul's call for abundance and joy. Anything that emerges from true inspiration arises for the best and comes out great. Knowing this is true wisdom!

If we were to condense all Modern Seers teaching into one simple instruction, then this Key Vortex "Relax, enjoy, and do something useful" is all you need to know. This Key Vortex contains all Modern Seers Teachings.

Action: Relax, enjoy, and do something useful!

2.2 Meditation practice

> Meditation is the tongue of the soul and
> the language of our spirit.
> — Jeremy Taylor

> Meditation brings wisdom;
> lack of mediation leaves ignorance.
> Know well what leads you forward
> and what hold you back,
> and choose the path that leads to wisdom.
> — Buddha

> Contemplation is to knowledge what digestion is
> to food — the way to get life out of it.
> — Tryon Edwards

Spiritual life "hangs" on meditation practice. Meditation practice is the engine that spurs a practitioner along the spiritual path. It is the heat that bakes the dough of spiritual growth into the bread of self-realization. Meditation practice permeates everything we do at Modern Seers. Hence, it is the second Universal Vortex.

Meditation is now mainstream. People and media talk about it. People take classes to learn it. Everyone knows it is good for you. Rediscovering what has been known for centuries, scientific research now confirms the "worldly usefulness" of meditation: it has a calming effect, balances blood pressure, has excellent stress reduction properties, and helps relax and control pain, to name a few. Meditation, however, has a deeper purpose that must not be trivialized.

Meditation is a form of spiritual practice. Let us take a look at the meaning of practice, spiritual, and (combined) spiritual practice.

Practice is a process through which we change a habitual state from undesirable to desirable. A habit of being uninformed can be changed to being well-informed by reading appropriate books. Being nervous about public speaking can be changed into composure and control through repeatedly giving public speeches.

In its purest form, we can observe practice in a baby learning to walk. The point of the practice is that the baby wants to move from a state of being a crawler to being an upright walker. He does not care about failure, falling, or immediate success. He is sure he will walk one day and he will. For that purpose, the baby attempts to walk persistently until she does.

Spirituality is about being connected to your inner self. It expresses itself in being passionately alive, peaceful within, connected to your unique spirit and life's mission. Spiritual practice is about connecting to that freedom, leaving the misery of being caught by and stuck in the mind.

Therefore, it is the mind that is the obstacle to be overcome through spiritual practice. The mind thinks, observes, and remembers. Accordingly, it remembers the past and thinks about the future in terms of the past. It limits you, even though it is useful precisely because it thinks, remembers, and plans. You may meet a very important person around the corner as you walk today to your office, but your mind will tell you not to pay attention because you have never met someone like this on your way to work before. The mind separates you from the alive and passionate You and pinches off the deep You with a collection of memories and habits that make up the shallow you.

The whole world is obsessed with such mental games. This drama is natural because humans are invested in their minds and attached to their thoughts. But the mind, while intelligent, is rarely wise. It can do very stupid things cleverly, like inventing nuclear power (clever) and then using nuclear arms (stupid).

Universal craziness is the fixation on being smart at the expense of being wise, the biggest human folly there is, and meditation is an effective medication against it. Meditation makes you ignore seemingly intelligent stupidity and see deeper wisdom.

Opening you up to the deeper You, meditation connects you to the amazing aliveness inside you. Meditation teaches you to greet every day as a new beginning and every moment as pregnant with new possibilities. Meditation opens you up to new opportunities that your mind cannot conceive of, but your wisdom is open enough to allow. This is called basic sanity, and meditation is a way to reach for it — in spite of living among people lost in their mental preoccupations, residing with them in their insane asylum called human society, hurt by their weird and senseless habits and tunnel vision, which they consider normal.

There are three kinds of meditation — respectively described at each Phase. All three address basic craziness and seek basic sanity. At Phase I, practice of insight meditation seeks to notice and to let go of the insanity. At Phase II, creative visualization meditation seeks to transform the madness into something more functional. At Phase III, direct meditation seeks experience of and stability in basic sanity. In order to understand any of these three "styles", we need experience — which happens through practice.

The *insight meditation* teaches being. It is about noticing where you are and how you are. It is about being here and now — in the present and not in the past or the future. It is about recognizing that past and future are mental projections that are conjured by the mind for its endless conceptualization processes.

Insight meditation leads to letting go — letting go of your resistance. Resistance to life is the root cause of all troubles, physical or mental. Humans are socialized to believe that making an effort is a way to success. Insight meditation teaches you to let go and let the flow of life take you toward success. That is why this seeming non-activity often generates so much inspiration for action and change.

The *creative visualization* meditation seeks to transform you directly into what you want to be. It engages the principle *as you think so you become.* This style of meditation is about pretending to be who you want to be — until you are no longer pretending. Practitioners typically imagine themselves to have appealing qualities such as peace, intuition, wisdom. After some practice, the practitioner begins to develop these qualities.

For example, it is natural to want to be near our role models because we seek to be like them. We naturally think of him or her and consequently derive pleasure and receive emotional sustenance from his or her company. We can spend time in the presence of the role model — or we can engage in visualization of being near him or her with similar results.

Likewise, if we meditate on peace, we will become peaceful in due time. If we visualize being a great writer, we will write better. Similarly, if we meditate on our inadequacies, we will attract them. Thus, the visualization meditation transforms by activating the *law of attraction*.

The topic of nondual or direct meditation is difficult (some say impossible) to talk about it without having a significant experience with the Phase I and Phase II meditation techniques. Thus, you will likely naturally discover direct meditation by the time you begin practicing Phase III Vortexes.

Meditation practice brings results regardless of how you are doing meditation, only regularity and patience are necessary. Daydreaming or fantasizing about possible results or worrying about whether you are or not meditating properly will only hinder the practice. The best way to begin meditation practice is simply to start, throwing all preconceived ideas out the window, including self-judging and worrying about the results.

Action: A meditation technique should be practiced twice a day, preferably before meals (but before one is hungry). Phase I students should practice insight meditation, Phase II students will practice creative visualization, and Phase III students will try nondual or direct meditation.

2.3 Engage teacher: Coaching and mentoring

> If you wish to know the road up the mountain,
> ask the man who goes back and forth on it.
> — Zenrin-kushū

> None but a guru can take a man
> out of the jungle of intellect and sense perceptions.
> So, there must be a guru.
> — Ramana Maharshi

> A teacher affects eternity;
> he can never tell where his influence stops.
> — Henry Adams

If you are interested in the deepest spirituality possible, you will recognize the need for having a teacher. The purpose of this Universal Vortex is to make you appreciate the need for the relationship and, more importantly, to let you gain the value from having the relationship.

If you are serious about acquiring spiritual depth, you will quickly realize that you cannot do it alone. In fact, the idea of going at it alone is one of the big delusions about the path, mostly entertained by Westerners scared of losing their independence — another big delusion.

The point to having a teacher is that his or her mentoring and coaching will help you accomplish what you want to accomplish efficiently, with the least pain possible. In fact, finding a competent spiritual teacher is the only real shortcut on the path that has no shortcuts.

This has been known for centuries. That is why a guru-disciple system exists in all societies where serious spiritual practice is valued. Negative beliefs about gurus are born of ignorance and suspicion of serious spirituality.

The guru-disciple system is not a uniquely Hindu or Buddhist concept. But theirs is perhaps the most developed and visible example of the system. Wise people in India, particularly along the Ganges valley and in the Himalayas, recognized the requirements necessary for effectively reaching for the deepest spirituality possible. A significant element of Indian society is serious about authentic spirituality and, therefore, does not play games with spiritual progress.

The key reason why the guru-disciple relationship is essential has to do with human nature. When we aspire to go beyond the false view of ourselves and wish to work with spiritual realities, our mind is both an obstacle and a helper. The mind's cleverness is both good and bad for you. To discern what is good (or bad) is difficult for the mind because it is, let us say, built in — it is your personality, it is you. Everything gets filtered through it. This is how people make mistakes — what feels good at the moment may not feel good in the future. What seems to work for you now may have unintended consequences, may not work later on.

Some authorities say that having a competent teacher is the difference between failure and success — keeping in mind that on the path of spirituality failures frequently look like trendy success. The mind has a great capacity to muddle things up. This is particularly because the mind has evolved as a short-term planning mechanism focused on survival as a tribe, not on what is best for you individually. Or for your spiritual evolution, which almost always is in opposition to the apparent needs of any society. Having a teacher who is more experienced, more spiritually developed, and emotionally more mature helps to navigate the way.

Life coaching and mentoring are two ways a modern guru serves you. As a mentor, he or she instructs you, and guides you in the direction you desire to go. As a life coach, he or she encourages positive action, which is the only way to discover who you are. The guru also creates space where you can experience yourself and let that real you inspire what you should do next in life.

Since a personal interaction between teacher and student should start early in the relationship, we suggest that students participate in group coaching or even start on personal coaching, beginning at Phase I.

Phase II students are recommended to participate in group coaching and are encouraged to benefit from individual coaching sessions. Phase III students are recommended to be coached individually and are encouraged to continue their participation in group coaching.

Both group and individual coaching sessions usually last 45-60 minutes and are conducted over the phone or in person. The commitment of twelve sessions is the recommended minimum to create a lasting change in your life. (More than 12 sessions may be necessary at times).

Action: A person serious about his or her spiritual evolution instinctively seeks help on the way. Take advantage of mentoring and coaching!

2.4 Retreats

> The Soul should always stand ajar
> That if the Heaven inquire
> He will not be obliged to wait
> Or shy of troubling Her...
> — Emily Dickinson

A retreat is a time you devote to exploring a new intensity and quality of being. It is a space where you step out of your normal circumstances and step into a new way and new perspective. At a retreat, you immerse yourself into the new paradigm — with the pointed intention of making the new state your permanent state. Engaging with Teaching through Retreats is the fourth Universal Vortex.

What is the state change we are talking about? Fundamentally, all spiritual practices are tools that provide instrumentation for leaving an ego-bound state in favor of becoming an adult. The ego-bound state, which is natural to childhood, becomes stuck and dysfunctional (i.e., quite unpleasant for you and others) beyond childhood. The adult-level Source-centered living is a free, open, and dynamic state when you let the Source (God) write the book of your life. You can be sure that Infinite Intelligence will do a better job at it than your limited ego. Almost all of the human population on our planet today suffers from the *emotional condition* of being a child — causing wars, economic crises, and other well-known ills that beset the world today.

It is hard to become an adult while being surrounded by children — but it can be done. A retreat is the best environment where you can see that there are other people who want to be adults. There is a big difference between merely knowing that such people exist and actually meeting and spending quality time with them. Seeing is believing that you are not alone in your quest!

To repeat, the key purpose of retreats is abandoning the stale, old ways in favor of new ways. The longer the duration of a retreat the more potential there is to permanently adopt or move to the new state. Of course, the duration to achieve permanent change depends on the person. Three to six months is typical to bring about a significant transformation – both by mentoring and coaching and through retreats.

Retreats are also a way for people of similar interests and intentions to focus energy. Retreats create an "incubator" effect, which can dramatically accelerate the speed of your practice. The incubator effect generates highly concentrated and well-focused synergy among the participants. Most group meditation periods during Modern Seers Retreats are used to deliberately increase the incubator effect.

Retreats at different Phases, while having much in common (and you are welcome to attend any and all), have different intentions. Retreats at Phase I are about tasting the experience. At Phase I, you should participate in one weekend retreat a year or more. Retreats at Phase II are about achieving understanding from a solid experience, about letting serious experience into your core. At Phase II, you should participate in two weekend retreats and one weeklong retreat per a year or more. Retreats at Phase III are about making a definitive move at staying at the new paradigm. At Phase III, you are expected to participate in four weekend retreats and two weeklong retreats per a year or more.

Short retreats are 2-3 days long, usually starting Thursday or Friday afternoon till Sunday morning (it ends after a brunch). Weeklong retreats last 7 days.

All of our retreats are relaxed. Intense purpose does not need to be tense. This is the reflection of the Key Vortex (Relax, enjoy, and do something useful) that enfolds everything we do at Modern Seers. The retreats revolve around group meditation periods, ample time for connecting with people, and healthy and tasty food, which is cooked so that you will never forget the experience. The schedule and topics reflect and are adjusted depending on the needs of the particular audience. Hence, *no two retreats are ever the same.*

A major part of spiritual endeavor is to conceive of higher living and then go there. A retreat serves both as a demonstration that the new paradigm exists and is reachable, and as an opportunity to become better established in the new world. The retreats are not a shortcut. Rather, the retreats are a concentrated, superfast way to accomplish real transformation.

Action: Attend retreats for the experience and the fastest way into the new paradigm.

3 Phase I Vortexes: Taste the experience

Courage is reckoned the greatest of all virtues;
because, unless a man has that virtue,
he has no security for preserving any other.
— Samuel Johnson

3.1 Relax, enjoy, and do something useful at Phase I

Your mind will answer most questions
if you learn to relax and wait for the answer.
— William S. Burroughs

I love Sufism as I love beautiful poetry,
but it is not the answer.
Sufism is like a mirage in the desert.
It says to you, come and sit,
relax and enjoy yourself for a while.
— Naguib Mahfouz

All good things in life start with taking it easy. Hence, the first Vortex, the Key Vortex that starts off Modern Seers teachings, calls us to relax. That is, at Phase I we will focus on the "relax" portion of the "relax, enjoy, do something useful" Vortex.

You can't really enjoy life if you are tense. You can't be deeply aware if you are worried. To put it bluntly, stressed out people miss quite a bit of their life. The spiritual path is fundamentally about finding your bliss, again and again, and going further every time. It is about tuning into the deeper part of you, your soul, where all the joy and satisfaction are found. You begin this process through relaxation because it increases your awareness. Haven't you noticed a new clarity after a nice stroll through a serene forest?

A relaxed state is a state with less tension. Stress is good in moderation — it calls for action, which is a great motivator. But most people today are too worried and too tense. Too much stress is a dysfunctional condition. This is mostly caused by fear-mongering leaders, greedy businesses, out-of-touch managers, and passive-aggressive public servants. All of these present the dire need for increased awareness and compassion for the fellow human beings in our society. The "job-holding" folks contribute to the problem through focusing on wrong priorities, which is also a problem of awareness.

Whatever state of grace or disgrace you are in right now, do find a few moments each day to tune into your tenseness and find a way to relax. You do not need a relaxation technique for this. The intention itself to lead a deliberately relaxed life will work fine. Insight meditation — or just sitting quietly as a technique in itself — is one of the most recommended ways into a more relaxed life. Meditation is an awareness practice — it will make you more aware of your priorities. Guess what the next Vortex will be!

Relaxation is ultimately an expression of trust that God is on your side, that Life will take care of you, that the Universe in due time will bring all the good stuff to you. All you need is to let go and let the magic take over.

Action: Take it easy — visit with your life.

3.2 Insight meditation

Practice meditation regularly.
Meditation leads to eternal bliss.
Therefore meditate, meditate.
— Swami Sivananda

If you want to find God,
hang out in the space
between your thoughts.
— Alan Cohen

Half an hour's meditation each day is essential,
except when you are busy.
Then a full hour is needed.
— Saint Francis de Sales

Insight meditation practice is the fundamental contemplative practice, which appears in various forms in all spiritual traditions. Simply put, it is a basic awareness practice. Becoming aware and doing something with the new knowledge that comes from the new realization (awareness), defines spiritual path. Spiritual evolution is about increasing awareness.

Here is a simple and effective method for insight style of meditation. Don't worry about other styles of insight meditation — they are all equally effective. Familiarize yourself with the following directions, so that you will not be distracted during your practice.

Sit comfortably on a chair, arm-chair, floor, mat or a blanket. Straighten your back. Put your hands on your lap one on top of the other (palms facing up), and close your eyes. Take three or four deep, slow breaths to relax a bit.

Slowly, step by step, direct your attention to all the major parts of the body. Start from your feet and finish at the crown of your head. Then, with an imaginary broom, sweep out the tension and fatigue starting at the bottom with your feet and finishing on top with your head. Then gradually let a feeling of pleasant relaxation enter the body, as if a vast seascape has opened up before you.

Now let into this inner seascape all of the inner and outer happenings — allow all the sounds, thoughts, perceptions and emotions to enter. DO NOT JUDGE OR ANALYZE THEM. Let these inner and outer happenings have a place inside you but do not dwell on them. Let them begin and end of their own accord without your participation.

Register the incessant chatter, fears, and hopes that continually surface in your consciousness. Note how you ceaselessly scheme about the future, thinking up projects that are unlikely to come to be. Feel the eternal itch of worry that something bad might happen. Listen to the lingering guilt about past mistakes. Open up inner space for these all to happen — both arise and retreat — as everything does in this world.

Start by doing this technique for 10-15 minutes once a day for the first couple weeks. Gradually increase the practice to 15-20 minutes twice a day.

Action: Practice the above technique.

3.3 Remember: Better and better!

> Once you replace negative thoughts with positive ones,
> you'll start having positive results.
> — Willie Nelson

This Vortex is about cutting negativity out of your life, and replacing it with a force of positive thinking. Since *'as we think so we become'*, since *'we create our own reality with our thoughts'*, this Vortex asks you to engage your mind and to think *better and better*. And — surprise, surprise — amazing things will start happening to you. Your life will get better.

For some weird evolutionary reasons, we humans tend to have a habit of negative thinking. This is an unconscious habit mostly. *Be prepared for the worst! It is bad and it will turn worse!* Numerous Murphy's Laws are the humorous examples we all have heard about.

But such thinking, while seemingly common sense, creates an inner environment that — engaging the *Law of Attraction* — will create external manifestations in due time. That is how people get in trouble, have accidents, fall sick, and have other negative experiences.

The alternative is to think that things will turn out well and will continue to get better. In other words, you should think that your life is becoming "better and better" — and it will start becoming so. Try it!

Positive thinking is powerful (and contagious). We become what we believe in. If you continuously tell yourself that things will get better, you will create a vortex of positivity and begin pulling positive results into your life.

Positive thinking, however, is not about lying to yourself, or about being unrealistic or naive. It is just a choice of thinking that glass is half full rather than half empty — which unblocks energy, allows things to flow, forward actions to happen — and this is the secret of achievement and success.

Of all the Vortexes, this one is one of the simplest to practice. But it works wonders when remembered with sincerity and determination. If we keep in mind that things tend to become better and better as we move along in life, we can relax and know in our hearts that we will be taken care of by the Universe, of which we are an integral part.

Action: Think "better and better" and your life will get better.

3.4 Day intending

I hope everyone that is reading this
is having a really good day.
And if you are not, just know that
in every new minute that passes
you have an opportunity to change that.
— Gillian Anderson

Our intention creates our reality.
— Wayne Dyer

We human beings are powerful creators. The intention of this Vortex is to begin training you to create the life you always wanted for yourself. It will introduce you to the limitless possibilities that open up for you, once you begin making an effort at living your life *deliberately*.

Creating your own reality is about synchronizing your wishes with the wishes the Universe (the Source or Divine Force) has for you. We humans are at a leading edge of Creation. Our genuine wishes are requests the Universe always fulfills. When our wishes do not come true, that is always because they are not genuine wishes. That means that (so far) we have not done a good job of learning what we really want.

In order to not get caught by the whining of the sort "Why didn't my wish for a new luxury car materialize instantly?" work on increasing the clarity of your intention. Work on separating your desires (what you truly want) from what others (parents, teachers, supervisors, traditions, etc.) want for you. And don't be disappointed if, after only a few weeks of practicing day intending, a day does not go exactly the way you wish. In every situation, your intention should be focused on what you want, rather than on *getting* what you want.

The practice: In this practice, you will focus on intending the day you want to live — as opposed to any particular part of the day. Before starting your day you will project your desire — and apply it for the whole day.

The practice itself goes as follows: In the morning, BEFORE you get out of bed, visualize the following: Imagine the most perfect day you could have. Be reasonable and realistic, but focus on the most positive and DETAILED outcome that you could have.

Examples of reasonable, realistic intentions: I will be more cheerful today than yesterday. I will feel more energy. I will have more clarity. People will mostly like me. There will be less stress today than yesterday.

Examples of unreasonable intentions: My day will be perfect. I will smile always. Everyone will like me. There will be only pleasant situations today. (Notice the perfectionism in these wishes. Perfectionists constrict rather than allow things to flow.)

If you forget to do the practice before getting out of bed, do the intending at the time you remember.

Action: Practice day intending every day and observe the results.

3.5 Mind influence of others

Tell me who your friend is and
I will tell you who you are.
— Russian proverb

Believe those who are seeking the truth;
doubt those who find it.
— André Gide

Some cause happiness wherever they go;
others whenever they go.
— Oscar Wilde

This Vortex calls you to become conscious of the influence people you meet have on you, and do something about it. This Vortex is about seeking out and engaging people who enrich you.

Humans are social beings, programmed by nature to survive as a group. The behavior of our tribe — be it friends or society in general — dictates our thoughts and shapes our personality. But the group seldom wants you to thrive as an individual; it only wants you to perpetuate survival of the group.

Your tribe does not care about your happiness and prosperity, unless it contributes to the tribe's survival, as defined by the common interests of the group. That is why social leaders constantly talk about the common good. But, as a truly spiritual person, you are interested in thriving, not merely surviving. You are, therefore, in natural opposition to the inherent mediocrity of your social environment.

Your thoughts define who you are and how you see the world around you. Your thoughts attract and define the reality you live. People you keep around, just like your language and culture, significantly influence your experience — without much conscious input on your part.

Since your social ecosystem contributes to your habits of thought, if you change your social environment, you change your thoughts. Seeking out people who enrich you is an easy way to change your life for the better without much effort.

Therefore, engaging people who are serious about bringing more awareness to their life is a time-tested, easy, and fun way of thoroughly improving your life. After all, people we meet influence us with their thoughts and their presence.

Remember the proverb: *Those who sleep with dogs will rise with fleas*. Why not socialize with the dogs infected with the *thrive and prosper* flees? It is really that simple!

Just like food offerings at a buffet diner, people you come in contact with in your daily life could be good, bad, and in between. It is up to you which dish you choose to eat! Thus, seek the company of good, positive people. Avoid your equals, for that will perpetuate the mediocrity the tribe wants for survival. Instead, seek out your betters — seek out the people you want to emulate.

Action: Choose your friends wisely.

3.6 Daily deposit

> There is a wonderful mythical law of nature that
> the three things we crave most in life —
> happiness, freedom, and peace of mind —
> are always attained by giving them to someone else.
> — Peyton Conway March

This Vortex is about making a daily deposit to your spiritual bank account, the account of Virtue. The size of your Virtue account determines the amount of Grace you receive. Grace makes your life run smoothly.

What is this *daily deposit*? It is doing something positive for someone without expecting anything in return — and preferably anonymously. It could be small like dusting your co-worker's desk, buying food for a sick neighbor, tutoring a neglected child, or fixing a friend's computer. It could be bigger such as volunteering for a worthwhile cause, giving most of your salary to an ashram, or dedicating your life to your Teacher's work. Of course, at Phase I you are only expected to do small deposits.

When you help someone spontaneously or deliberately, you receive a blessing from their soul. The more good deeds you do the more Virtue is deposited to your "good karma" bank account, and the more "good luck" you will experience. You may experience the Grace as your perspective expanding, your life running more smoothly, or simply feeling better.

A deeper explanation of the Grace and Virtue link is found in the Law of Cause and Effect ("as you sow, so shall you reap") that operates at the Causal Level of the Universe. Regular daily "contributions" of Virtue are a way to control the timing of the "reaping" by relieving yourself of your karmic burden on your own schedule.

That is why those who give their life to spiritual service tend to be the happiest people. They know that large deposits of Virtue always bring about abundant Grace.

Anonymously or not, helping others makes you a better person and works on removing negative habits in favor of positive ones. Doing good is good, period.

Action: Nourish your soul — deposit virtuous deeds into your spiritual bank account every day.

3.7 Uplifting mind-food

> I always turn to the sports section first.
> The sports section records people's accomplishments.
> The front page has nothing but man's failures.
> — Earl Warren

This Vortex asks you to consume what is good for you by becoming conscious of beneficial nourishment, particularly thoughts, that you let in.

We consume not only food but thoughts — the thoughts we think, the thoughtforms we receive from our social environment, from the books we read, the news we pay attention to, the company we keep around us, etc.

Mind-food enters us and affects us. As a rule, good nourishment makes you feel good emotionally (happy), while taking it in, and afterward. Knowing what feels good presumes a certain degree of awareness on your part. Leaving what feels bad and seeking out what feels good implies an ability to make things happen in your life — leaving bad habits by forming good habits.

To engage this Vortex, read uplifting books, watch positive videos, meet with people who make you feel better. What thoughts inspire and uplift you and the specific way you might introduce the positive thoughtforms into your mind (books, videos, people?) is an individual decision.

Avoid taking in thoughtforms that are geared toward the general public because all cultures today are negatively oriented, even though they might appear otherwise on the surface. The main problem is that cultures present you with limited choice, which they cloak as the only available options. The biggest offenders today are watching TV in general, and consuming negative TV news in particular. The same goes for most print media.

(You should definitely be well-informed, but this can be done in minutes by browsing a few of the news sites on the Internet. There is no need to spend hours watching negative programs on TV, particularly if they make you go upstream.)

Gradually phase out regular consumption of irrelevant or negative mind-food. Make an effort to consume uplifting, nutritious thoughts, just as you should consume healthy food. It is amazing how people who would never eat rotten food have no problem letting in bad thoughts. Thus, focus on the good mind-food.

Eventually you will regain your ability to ignore bad mind-food, just like you avoid food that smells rotten. One of the best ways to increase the intake of better thoughts and emotions is engaging a Teacher as mentor or life coach.

Action: Seek out what nourishes you emotionally and intellectually.

3.8 Coaching: Consider

> The greatest happiness of life is the conviction that
> we are loved — loved for ourselves,
> or rather, loved in spite of ourselves.
> — Victor Hugo

At Phase I, we are not expecting that you engage a mentor or a life coach. Rather, it is a time for considering what it would be like to have a relationship with the best friend you can have. By practicing these Vortexes, you are already engaging Teacher — even though engaging Teacher formally will happen at the later Phases.

Engaging a teacher or a teaching is perhaps a strange concept; even though we have no cultural problem with sending children to school, or studying medicine, anthropology, or another advanced discipline. We worry about a Teacher messing with our mind or our independence — all while letting culture, education, and religion mess with our mind and our independence.

Phase I is the time of exploring the *'Is this for me?'* question. It is a time to have a serious look at yourself and ask, *Am I in control or does someone else have control over my life?* It is a time to consider if sporadic thoughts about becoming healthy in the body, agile in the mind, and radiant in your spirit are good enough, or if having a time-tested support system — with Teacher, Teachings, and peers helping you along the way, would be better. Isn't this why you came upon these Vortexes (and teachings) in the first place?

At Phase I, it is expected that you work on committing to yourself first. Consider what happens when you follow the values and ideals of someone, someone who cannot possibly know your values and your principles (unless they enter and become you). Ask yourself, *Am I committed to me or am I loyal to someone else?* and *How can a commitment to someone else possibly help me?* As you understand the difficulty of committing to you, you will understand the value of having the best *best friend* whose singular professional purpose is to make you focus on being committed to yourself.

   Action: Visualize the best friend whose job is to make you commit to what is the best for you through mentoring and life coaching.

3.9 Retreats at Phase I: Taste

> To be surprised, to wonder,
> is to begin to understand.
> — José Ortega y Gasset

> Joy is not in things, it is in us.
> — Charles Wagner

A retreat is a time spent away from your regular life for the purpose of reconnecting with the deeper you. Retreats are opportunities to intensify and deepen your practice, and to meet people like you.

At a Phase I retreat, we want you to have a good time — enjoy your meditation, eat fun food, meet interesting people who are curious about the same thing as you are, make a few good friends, encounter new ideas. We want you to taste a deeper and richer spiritual experience.

Good things happen when you are with a group of people moving through a similar practice and experience. Spiritual energy that builds is greater than the energy of the individuals meditating alone. This is due to the "incubator" effect, the special synergy that develops among individuals in the group. The "incubator" effect helps deepen your practice without any significant effort of your own. It is an easy way to achievement — and a big reason for participating in retreats. There is also a bit of a natural peer pressure to go deeper.

Phase I students are recommended to attend one weekend (short) retreat a year, or more. Short retreats are 2-3 days long, usually starting Thursday or Friday afternoon and lasting until Sunday morning. The retreat ends after a delicious brunch. Phase I students are also welcome to attend a weeklong retreat if they wish.

You can do as many Phase I retreats as you like. This is because every retreat will be different, because each group brings their own special energy to practice, discussions, and experiences. So, repeating is not repetitious.

Action: Attend one or more weekend retreats a year.

4 Phase II Vortexes:
Go beyond tasting

We don't think about pilgrimage in this country.
We don't think about meditation.
The idea of taking a six-week walk is
totally foreign to most Americans.
But it's probably exactly what we need.
— Emilio Estevez

4.1 Relax, enjoy, and do something useful at Phase II

> Not what we have but what we enjoy
> constitutes our abundance.
> — Epicurus

> True happiness is to enjoy the present,
> without anxious dependence upon the future.
> — Lucius Annaeus Seneca

> Time you enjoy wasting was not wasted.
> — John Lennon

At Phase II, let's focus on the "enjoy" part of the Key Vortex "relax, enjoy, and do something useful".

The primal yearning of every living being in this world is to enjoy its life, to "follow your bliss". All human activity has "seek more pleasure" as its inspiration — we all long for feeling better in the future. This is natural because we human beings at our core are divine beings having a bodily experience. We are eternal, blissful souls incarnating in a physical body.

Our soul — being positively focused — in its essence is about joy, satisfaction, and peace. It does not forget its blissful nature even when identified with a particular body and mind. Even if you are busy making a living, you still have to do the enjoyment thing. Otherwise, you will pinch yourself away from the natural happiness inside you and become miserable, and we see such people every day. Money, power, relationships, enlightenment, and the new sofa in your living room are tools that help you enjoy life. They are not joy in and of themselves — joy is independent from owning or having stuff.

We get joy from connecting to our real self in each moment. No happiness "tool" in the wide world can help you unless you relax into the present moment and actually stop, notice, focus on the moment — and actually savor it. We have fun by being playful and taking our life lightly. We get happy and satisfied by focusing on and savoring the present moment. Yes, you can be mature and responsible as well as playful and happy.

How to enjoy? Begin by paying more attention to where your joy is and by following your bliss. We enjoy by savoring the present moment, which is only fully possible if you are relaxed, see this Key Vortex at Phase I. You do it actually tasting the food when eating, delighting in the pillow when you sleep, enjoying your friends when you are with them (by focusing on them and ignoring your beeping smart phone). You do the enjoying by actually living your life to the fullest — by thriving and delighting with being alive, rather than surviving. And this brings us to the next point I wish to make.

Frequently, real joy is replaced with hopeful thoughts of potential joy in the future, a common spiritual malady. Hope is good but it is not about being focused on and enjoying the present moment. Hope is about the future. We stop the hope delusion by facing our desire to enjoy life and be happy now. We observe how our mind tricks us into believing that the future will bring us something. All work, all thinking, all business activity is motivated by this hope — a mostly false belief that we will become happy and satisfied one day through a lot of effort. But by that time your idea of happiness and satisfaction will evolve beyond your current wisdom — or beyond what traditionally is considered proper.

Most people today could use more joy and less stress. Yet, all cultural traditions civilize our joys and pains. They dictate how we are allowed to enjoy and what are "responsible" or "desirable" pleasures. Closely linked to cultural traditions are religious ideologies, and those broadcast "values" that are suspicious of real joy and — overtly or covertly — encourage bogus happiness — the happiness of good looks that conceals pain and dissatisfaction of the soul, whose longing for freedom has been curtailed by narrow beliefs. At this Vortex Phase II, it is good to start having a good look at such beliefs and "received" ideologies and to begin challenging them. Therefore, let this Vortex summon you toward reclaiming joy and fun from externally imposed ideas or your own preconceived notions.

Action: Savor your body, senses, moods, mind, and spirit. Isn't this what we came here for?

4.2 Creative visualization meditation

> To visualize is to see what is not there,
> what is not real — a dream.
> To visualize is, in fact, to make visual lies.
> Visual lies, however, have a way of coming true.
> — Peter McWilliams

> Ordinary people believe only in the possible.
> Extraordinary people visualize
> not what is possible or probable,
> but rather what is impossible.
> And by visualizing the impossible,
> they begin to see it as possible.
> — Cherie Carter-Scott

> The mind is everything.
> What you think you become.
> — Buddha

Creative visualization seeks to introduce a new, better way of living and being by introducing new, more functional thoughtforms into your mind. At Phase II, you will experiment with six creative visualization techniques.

Thoughtforms are mental habits. We know them as beliefs, attitudes, and values. We seldom examine them because we consider such thinking normal and sensible. Thoughtforms dictate to us what is reasonable and what is possible. You are unlikely to ever be happy if you believe happiness is not possible for most people. You will not likely have a meaningful life if you believe your life should not have meaning. If you run a mental recording constantly saying that you will fail, guess how much success will come to you? To quote Wayne Gretzky, "You miss 100 percent of the shots you never take."

Thought patterns (thoughtforms) that limit us come from two major sources. The external causes are the thoughts that were imposed on us by our culture, religion, history, and family. The internal causes are the thoughts that were useful to us when we were younger but may not be functional when we are older and more experienced.

Creative visualization techniques are a way of going beyond our limited thinking by working with your mind through your imagination. Through a relentless, disciplined practice, the techniques persistently introduce new thought patterns.

At Phase I, you have developed the disciplined practice of insight meditation and developed some insight into your thought patterns. No doubt, these insights have already instigated you to alter your thought habits. At Phase II, you will attempt to dislodge these thought patterns even further.

Practicing creative visualization further sensitizes you to the thoughtforms you carry around with you. The practice opens your mind and dares you to think bigger and better — toward rising above your own self-imposed limitations, toward the remarkable person you can become. No, it is not a gimmick that Modern Seers people dare themselves and each other to be all they can be!

Below, are six transformational visualization techniques for you to try out. It might be a good idea to do a different technique each day for six days in a week and then on the seventh day either take a day off or repeat the technique you like the most.

After each visualization, take a note of your thoughts: write them in a journal, discuss them with a friend, your mentor, or with yourself. Record how you feel. Did you experience anything special or unusual? Did you enjoy the technique, and why? How are your life and thoughts affected by these practices? Share why these techniques helped you (if they did).

Splendid life visualization: Visualize yourself in your "next" life, the new life you want. Make that new life perfect in every way — in a very detailed manner. Visualize in great detail the house you will live in and its location, the friends you will have, the partner you will have, the parents you will be born to, the job you will especially enjoy, the size of your bank accounts, etc. The point of this visualization is to imagine the best you possible — the best potential for you in this life. (Don't get hung up on whether there is reincarnation, etc.)

Great friend visualization: Visualize a great, very special friend visiting you. This friend is very loving, very caring, and understands you perfectly. He or she came to visit you because he or she has a special message for you — a message of joy and love. Have a conversation with the friend. Tell him or her all you need to tell (don't dwell on the negative). Let the friend coach you toward feeling better and better — until you begin to feel really wonderful, joyful, loving toward yourself. The point of this visualization is to learn to love yourself better.

Hug a younger self visualization: Visualize yourself hugging a younger you, then repeat your own name to yourself encouragingly and with love — like a really perfectly loving parent would do. Use the name that you like to call yourself best; it does not have to be your given name. This is especially effective if you are experiencing a trouble of some sort. Imagine hugging yourself before the trouble started. Encouragingly guide yourself through the struggle, always visualizing the best possible outcome at each point. The point of this exercise is to relax into the natural you, which is loving, encouraging, positive, and life-affirming.

Omnipotent self visualization: Visualize yourself as an omnipotent being. Imagine that you are capable of everything and anything. How will you change yourself and influence others near you? What will you create for and in the world?

Royal visualization: Visualize yourself as a king or queen of the land. You are an autocratic but benevolent ruler. Everyone always obeys you because they know you are both powerful and just. What will you make your subjects do? Be genuine with your desires, remember this is a visualization.

Peaceful corner visualization: Visualize yourself in the best, most peaceful, pleasant place you can be. A beach, a mountain top, a fragrant forest? Imagine lying on a comfortable bed or on the cool grass, or sitting in a comfortable chair or armchair — enjoying the place, gradually relaxing until you are completely at peace and in love with life. Stay in that state for a while. The point of this is to teach you that your perspective (attitude) always starts from within.

Action: Practice each visualization for fifteen to twenty minutes. Doing the same technique two times the same day might be a good idea as well.

4.3 Avoid upstream thinking

> You've got to win in your mind
> before you win in your life.
> — John Addison

> A man's errors are his portals of discovery.
> — James Joyce

Any situation that presents itself to us can elicit a resistant or allowing response from us. You can offer thoughts that open you to life, or that close you to the experience. We can choose between the two thoughts. This Vortex draws your awareness to this fact.

The stream of life is akin to the powerful current of a river. You cannot paddle upstream for too long before you become tired. The river (of life) will take you downstream eventually. Thus, downstream thinking directs thoughts in the positive direction, in the direction of allowing, in the direction of what you want to happen. Upstream thinking is resistant, blocking, not allowing. It thinks "what I want will never happen" thoughts.

Both upstream and downstream thinking are just thinking. Thinking is not an action that could follow, or predicting events that may or may not happen. Thus, upstream thinking is dysfunctional by its very nature. It is a strange way of avoiding disappointment with some future event. It asserts that you will fail and, therefore, should not try. Upstream thinking directs you to maim your foot because you are afraid to walk.

Some people are naturally positive, others are not. Most cultures in the world encourage the dysfunctional upstream thinking. Negative thinking is one of the natural ways the human ego, which is very fragile and easily hurt, protects itself. (A strong-willed person is in tune with his or her soul-strength. This allows him or her to ignore his or her ego's pettiness and fragility.)

The practice of the Vortex: In each situation, consciously choose a thought that makes you feel better. Choose the best response your mind can offer to the event. The key to engaging this Vortex is becoming more aware of upstream thinking. This will naturally result in more downstream thinking.

For example, you have a bill to pay but you currently don't have the money. You can think "I never have enough money. I am such a bad earner. I am a terrible person." Or you can think "I have a temporary problem with money. But I am working on it. A new client might call today. I have always paid my bills on time before." Notice how one stream of thinking is reactive and resistant, and another is consciously positive and allowing. One opens you up to receiving and another closes you down to receiving.

Downstream thinking is not about lying to yourself. There is a difference between being in denial and being both positive and realistic. This Vortex entices you to think the most positive thought you can under the circumstances — without lying to yourself. Lying to yourself is phony and is not what this Vortex is about. We are not talking here about sham affirmations.

Notice the difference between the following statements: "After that terrible blog post by that no good writer, my business will fail." "No one has noticed the bad publicity. My business will continue to thrive." "My company was hurt but we have been through more trying times and know how to recover." Or another set: "I have cancer and will die." "I don't have cancer because my doctor is wrong." "The diagnosis is serious but the doctor believes I will be cured." Or one more: "I will fail the exam because I am stupid." "The teacher likes me — I will pass." "I have succeeded many times and, even though this exam is hard, I will study hard without worrying too much about the outcome."

Also, note that resistance can be very subtle and so can be allowing. Many times engaging a life coach is helpful for determining if your thinking is upstream or downstream.

Action: Become aware of upstream thinking.

4.4 Period intending

No great man ever complains of want of opportunity.
— Ralph Waldo Emerson

Every moment of your life is infinitely creative and
the Universe is endlessly bountiful.
Just put forth a clear enough request and
everything your heart desires must come to you.
— Shakti Gawain

Love does not obey our expectations;
it obeys our intentions.
— Lloyd Strom

By now, you must have had a bit of intuition and experienced some manifestations that indicate that you are a powerful creator who is waiting to uncover and awaken his or her ability. With this Vortex, your experiments with projecting positive intention will continue and become more concrete and specific. This Vortex aims to bring more consciousness to the process.

The secret to creating your own reality is realizing that every wish is fulfilled in this Universe — if we only learn how to let go and allow it. Most people are great generators of desires, but are terrible at allowing these wishes to be fulfilled. That is, most of us have many desires that are waiting to be fulfilled. That is why clarifying a wish and making it concrete in your mind is essential to experiencing wish fulfillment. Since all our wishing is ultimately about making ourselves feeling better, this process teaches us to go in the direction of feeling better — having better life.

In this practice, instead of doing intending for a day, you will apply intending to each *period* of your day. A period or a segment is a circumscribed part of the day. For example, a morning time — shower, breakfast, and dressing up for work — is a period. Arriving at your place of work, working, and then leaving for home is another segment. Your evening meditation is another period. Night sleep is one more example.

Each period can be further divided into sub-periods, depending on their importance to you. For example, a part of your workday when you have an important conversation with your supervisor (a salary increase, no?) is a segment worth intending for by itself.

The technique: The actual technique is very simple. Before entering the period, intend how you want the period to go and surrender into your desire. Visualize your desire already fulfilled and focus on the feeling you have after the desire has been fulfilled. Imagine the most perfect situation during the period you could have. Be reasonable and realistic but focus on the most positive outcome you could have.

If you forget to do the practice before the period starts, do the intending at the time when you remember.

Action: Practice Period Intending every day and note the results.

4.5 Pain body

Young souls learn to accept
responsibility for their actions.
Mature souls learn to accept
responsibility for their thoughts.
And old souls learn to accept
responsibility for their happiness.
— Mike Dooley

Pain body is the cause of human drama. This Vortex draws
you in toward awareness of your pain body. The awareness
disarms it.

Pain body is a part of the human ego that stores negative
experiences and reacts to new situations based on those
experiences. These reactions become "hard-wired" into the
"unconscious" as undesirable tendencies in personal, family,
tribal, national, professional, etc. situations. These hardened
emotional pathways are a burden. They make you an automaton,
mindlessly reacting to new situations in the old ways. But the past
does not define the future.

Painful emotions, if unprocessed, build up in individual and
collective psyche. The pain body takes on a life of its own and
inserts itself in every situation, creating instability and causing
drama. Your pain body attracts events and people who will feed it,
increase its size, and confirm its existence. Thus, the hater meets
the hated and a victimizer finds her victim — both are activations
of their pain bodies.

Human beings are not good at processing their negative
experiences. The processing involves the unpleasantness of
recollecting and reliving the old painful events. Most people
prefer to bury the baggage, even though they know that sweeping
the dirt under the carpet does not make the room clean.

The key to disarming the pain body is not feeding it. Pain
body lives on new experiences that validate its old emotional

pathways. You have to break the cycle by becoming aware — monitoring — how your perceptions are guided by your pain body. Increasing awareness is key here.

I know two friends, a German and a Jew. The Jewish man has moved on from fearing every German because his or her grandfather might have been a criminal in the Holocaust. But the German man is still ashamed of the deeds he has not done. The two cannot freely enjoy each other because there is an old skeleton in one of the closets. The functional way would be to admit to the horrible past and vow to never repeat it — and move on.

When you become aware of your pain body, the old "memories" no longer control your current behavior. You have the alternative of choosing a new behavior that is more appropriate to the new situation.

Action: Become aware of your pain body. Avoid feeding it.

4.6 Engage Teacher: Experience

Spirituality is not a course in literature.
— Stewart Brinton

God holds each of us by a string.
When we sin, we cut the string.
But God ties it up again, making a knot.
Each time our wrong doing cuts the string,
God ties another knot — drawing us up closer to Him.
— Meister Eckhart

You identify yourself with the body
you think that the Guru is also a body.
You are not the body, nor is the Guru.
You are the Self and so is the Guru.
This knowledge is gained by what you call Self-realization.
— Ramana Maharshi

At Phase II, the Universal Vortex "Coaching" invokes the intention to experience working with Teacher. Thus, we recommend you to enroll in group coaching. We also encourage you to try individual life coaching, if you wish.

As you may well know, knowledge cannot be theoretical to be real. You must apply knowledge to make it real. That is why at this Phase we want you to stop thinking about it and actually engage Teacher and experience. The purpose here is to engage Teacher in order to have an experience, so that you will have some real knowledge in order to make intelligent choices.

Teacher creates an open, safe space for you to experience deeper parts of you. Imagine having interactions with someone who knows real love and really loves you — wants the best for you on all levels! Imagine conversing with someone who has your best interests in his mind all the time, whose energy is uplifting, who will infuse happiness in you, who will reorient you to view every situation from the most positive perspective possible at each moment. Imagine finding more clarity about direction of your life!

This is not hype but the role of Teacher in your life. A Teacher is defined by students. Students are the ones who evoke the best from Teacher and are capable of receiving and, therefore, benefitting from Teachings. Genuine Teacher-Student relationship is inspiring for both!

Enrolling into a group coaching class implies "graduation" from Phase I to Phase II. At Phase II, you are recommended to complete twelve group coaching sessions. This may also be accomplished by enrolling into the Shining Being Training, which includes twelve group coaching session as a part of the program.

At Phase II, you may also participate in individual coaching but this is not suggested or expected. And do not be too eager for individual coaching. Group coaching is very effective, and it eases you gradually into realizing the value of coaching for you. If you do decide to go for individual coaching, make sure to stick with it until all 12 sessions are completed.

Action: Open your heart and mind to experience the twelve sessions of group coaching.

4.7 Balanced life

> He who lives in harmony with himself,
> lives in harmony with the world.
> — Marcus Aurelius

Balanced life is about bringing harmony to the conflicting priorities in your life. It is about dealing with conflicting authenticities. We are not always entirely conscious of the various expressions that make us up. Our body, mind, intellect, creativity, work, vocation, relationships — each seek their true selves, their authentic expression.

To better understand what a balanced life is (and before you go any further), do an exercise: Consider how you manage your many expressions. Are you running a democracy, an autocracy, a constitutional monarchy, a theocracy, or an anarchy in your head? How do you treat your constituents? Which part of you is the ruler of the roost? Do you suppress some or most of your "parts" or put a tight lid on just one? Do you let one, some, or all loose?

Here are a few more questions to ponder and bring to awareness: Do you treat our body with respect? Do you believe that a healthy body is the gateway to having a fruitful, peaceful, content life? How do you treat your animal instincts, fears, sex-drive, and appetite for food?

How do you treat your intellect? Do you appreciate your capacity to think? How do you expand your thinking? Meditation, prayer, reading, travel? Do you perpetuate unexamined beliefs that were passed down to us by our parents or our ethnic group?

How do you treat our creativity? Do you stuff it under the rug for being spontaneous, unruly and irrational? Do you know the difference between irrational and transrational?

When was the last time you communed with a creek, hugged a tree, said thank you to a blade of grass while walking in a pristine forest? Do you admire this amazing Divine Creation?

Finally, among all these aspects of your life, which one are you most passionate about? Body, mind, emotions, creativity, relationships, God? What is your passion? Do you like your passion? Do you fight with it?

In the battle of authenticities, various aspects of you compete for your attention. Who wins out is the key question on the spiritual path. Will it be the intellect, your social self, emotions, the body? What part of you is the most important to you?

Action: Strive to lead a balanced life yourself. Encourage everyone to lead a balanced life.

4.8 Be yourself

> Be yourself — everybody else is already taken.
> — Oscar Wilde

A common spiritual malady is pretending to be someone else in hopes of being accepted by others. A bad boy, a good girl, a bohemian artist, a loving wife, a future Buddha — all could be personas that we adopt to impress others. Through this Vortex, you will go beyond these personas.

By adopting a false persona we invite acceptance and love toward a mask — a false image we create for the benefit of eliciting positive responses from others. Yet, we want love and acceptance of our real selves, not fake selves. The result is loneliness and hunger for love — often amidst seemingly great popularity. Most humans suffer from this malady to some extent but celebrities and politicians are particularly prone to it (because their popularity depends on their public image).

We lie about ourselves because we do not believe deep down we are lovable the way we are. Yet, we seek unconditional love in spite of our habits, behaviors, looks. Ultimately, we seek spiritual practices such as these Vortexes to get in touch with that Universal Love.

A false persona is disrespectful, an affront toward Nature (God). If you were meant to be someone else, you would be created as that someone else. To use a "western religious" language, the biggest sin that could possibly be committed is not accepting how God made you — because it is rejecting God's Will. The purpose of your life is found in using your gifts. He made you the way you are!

Relaxing into who you are starts with accepting where you are now. It involves gradually becoming aware and letting go of externally imposed judgments about yourself that you unconsciously accepted. An insight meditation practice helps engaging this Vortex; it helps with learning what is and isn't authentic you.

See the Vortex "Authenticity" for a complementary view of the topic, on page 82.

Action: Be yourself: Tell the truth about yourself so that others can know you and love you the way you are.

4.9 Retreats at Phase II: Experience

> You cannot acquire experience by making experiments.
> You cannot create experience. You must undergo it.
> — Albert Camus

> Some people drink from the fountain of
> knowledge, others just gargle.
> — Robert Anthony

At Phase II, it is your time to go beyond tasting — toward a solid experience of the new paradigm. At this point, you are now done simply checking out what Modern Seers is, and are now beginning to ponder if the ways of Modern Seers are for you — if the intention of those engaged with the organization is close to your own essential intention. Thus, you now have the agenda and you want to confirm that you feel at home with Modern Seers folks.

If your soul's journey is intimately connected with Modern Seers, you have found your spiritual home, your spiritual safe heaven. Keep in mind that this is not a decision that your ego should make. The conclusion should emerge from your innermost self, your soul — and come naturally in its due time. This Retreat Vortex and all other Vortexes are just a way to help shine light to you on what is obvious to your soul and in the process clarify to you what you really want and where your journey should take you. Ultimately, all paths are about becoming committed to awakening to your own life.

Another thing that you will get from the people conducting the retreat is a support and love that you cannot get anywhere else. Meeting people who strive to love and support you at your deepest level is no longer a miracle but still quite rare. You cannot get this kind of love from your family, because they simply do not provide the love you need for the spiritual path. Love of parents tends to be worldly and possessive, while the love of Modern Seers is opening you up and allowing you to thrive as who you truly are — as the authentic you. This support is very important particularly while making the transition into a spiritual life. That is what we provide during these retreats. It is an open and accepting love, and an open space for growth.

Phase II students are recommended to attend two weekend (short) retreats and one weeklong retreat per a year or more. Short retreats are 2-3 days long, usually starting Thursday or Friday afternoon till Sunday morning (ends after a brunch). Weeklong retreats last 7-10 days.

Action: Attend two weekend retreats and one weeklong retreat per a year or more.

5 Phase III Vortexes: Confirm the experience

All men dream, but not equally.
Those who dream by night
in the dusty recesses of their minds
wake in the day to find that all was vanity;
but the dreamers of the day are dangerous men,
for they may act their dream with open eyes,
and make it possible.
— Lawrence of Arabia

5.1 Relax, enjoy, and do something useful at Phase III

> The outward work will never be puny
> if the inward work is great.
> — Meister Eckhart

> Happy people plan actions, they don't plan results.
> — Denis Waitley

> The main thing to do is relax and let your talent do the work.
> — Charles Barkley

At Phase III, we will focus on "do something useful", the last part of the Key Vortex. The purpose of "doing something useful" should be self-evident, for most people are obsessed with doing what they think "useful" actions are. At Phase III, this Vortex is about learning to act after tuning to the deepest you, only after relaxing and enjoying, instead of first acting and them attempting to relax and enjoy. Then action comes from inspiration, rather than perspiration (motivation). This is likely the only "big" philosophy that you will ever need to completely transform your life.

Why must "relax" and "enjoy" come before "do something useful"? Early on in their lives, people develop a habit of scheming for the future. This restless mental planning is based on their interpretation of their past experiences. This habit shifts attention away from the present moment, the only moment when we experience — and enjoy — our life. The present moment is where the enjoyment we so diligently seek occurs. We miss the experience of enjoyment by disassociating ourselves from the present moment by thinking about the past and the future.

At Phase III, you need to reverse this trend by making a decision of relaxing into the present moment first, finding the most pleasant thought you can under the circumstances (which will point you toward your bliss), and only then doing something.

In fact, relax and enjoy first — because the inspiration to do something useful will naturally come to you when you are peaceful and enjoying your life.

Let me deflate hope a bit. Hope is a positive emotion that occurs when one is dreaming about the future — another distraction from the present moment. Doing something useful now is a way to channel your hope habit into the present moment by creating a momentum, a forward movement toward what you truly desire, toward more enjoyment.

Action: At each moment, relax, enjoy — and create a forward movement in your life by doing something concrete toward manifesting your desires.

5.2 Nondual meditation

> The consciousness in you and the consciousness in me,
> apparently two, really one, seek unity and that is love.
> – Nisargadatta Maharaj

Before we introduce nondual meditation style, let's take a brief look at what dual and nondual approaches are. When we identify with the temporal — mind, body and emotions — we are in duality. When we know that we are God or Eternal Soul manifesting in human form we are in nonduality.

Humans who truly fathom nonduality are extremely rare, for they are the true emissaries of Divine Beyond. Duality is the common state of human beings. We think we are separate from Nature and God. We feel that God helps us and punishes us, which are all dual approaches. In dual meditation, we apply a technique or several in hope that by a certain manipulation of our mental states we can move toward God. And it appears so — because we get some help. Our minds get calmer and our bodies healthier with meditation. Even the science of meditation shows that.

But those dual approaches do not solve the big problem. We still fear. This fear is a manifestation of our innate knowledge that we are immortal, which ego usually successfully highjacks. But ego is all about me and them, this and that. Such is mortal duality. Our body and mind will die. Ego hates that and installs itself as the "immortal" impostor, giving birth to endless manifestations of spiritual materialism.

(In the West, we call this impostor the Satan, from the Hebrew Ha-Satan, which translates as "the accuser", or "the adversary". Thus, anything that blocks free flow of energy would be Satan...)

Once we realize that we are immortal, we begin to see that our ego is just a temporary manifestation — a chemical reaction, if you may, in the body, which is also mortal. We begin to focus on the Eternal. We begin to live in nonduality. Then we know that we will never die — because we have direct knowledge that we are Cosmic Consciousness (God or Source Energy). In this realization, we gain complete and ultimate freedom — we reach the goal of all religions, of all spiritual practices.

But initially and for a few years we will swing between duality and nonduality, even though we know we are Eternal Souls. A part of us will still occasionally (and quite frequently in the initial stages) cling to the mortal or dual mind and body. Nondual meditation addresses this clinging. In nondual meditation, we remind ourselves that we are God and attempt to stay for a while in this natural state.

Nondual meditation has many historical instances. Mahamudra, Dzogchen, and Abhidhyana Yoga (our traditional system) are the nondual approaches. A nondual meditation will not make real sense until we begin to lose our identification with the dual. Thus, for many of you this Vortex will seem strange and premature — and thus should be practices as an interesting playful exercise. We included it at this Phase because everything we do in Modern Seers ultimately originates from nondual realization, and we thought you should know about it.

Action: During your usual meditation practice period, visualize yourself as an Eternal Being, a Buddha or Christ Consciousness, free from death and dying, ever alive, manifesting Itself as this amazing and surprising Universe, full of various forms, such as animals and plants, stones and rivers, humans good and evil, good and bad events — all being an eternal display of God's power to create forever.

5.3 Become friendly with the present moment

Look at everything as though you were seeing it
either for the first or last time.
Then your time on earth will be filled with glory.
— Betty Smith

"Someday" may never come.
So live each day better than the last.
That way you'll wake up with
so much excitement and anticipation
you'll jump out of bed and shout "I can't wait!"
— Bob Perks

Plenty of people miss their share of happiness, not because
they never found it, but because they didn't stop to enjoy it.
— William Feather

If you have not realized through a meditation practice or
directly, "we are" and "we experience" are the only true
statements. The rest is fiction — important fiction but fiction
nonetheless. This Vortex draws you to awareness of this
innermost knowledge.

What does that mean — that everything but the present is
fiction? Our memories of the past are thoughts. Can you be sure
that the past really happened? Can you be sure the past is more
than collective thoughtforms we all share together, share in the
now, thinking them in the present moment?

How about the future? Is future anything more than a
thought? Is scheming about the future more than just a mental
projection — a mental habit — for using your perceptions and
past experiences to imagine events yet to come — which, just like
thoughts about your past, are also just thoughts in the present?
Thus, if you set your cultural conditioning and mental habits aside,
all you have really ever going for you is the present moment.

Why do we need to be in the present moment? Our constant dwelling in, scheming about the future, angling for the best piece of the pie we can get is a good thing. Without mentally creating the future, we could not, nor would we live up to our potential. The problem, though, is that we experience and enjoy life in the present now. When we worry about the past and scheme about the future, we fail to consider that each moment is new and will never repeat itself ever again. Each moment is where the joy of living is experienced. The present moment is where you live, where you are alive. You are a spark of consciousness that always dwells in the present moment. The present moment is who you are.

Becoming friendly with the present moment is becoming friendly with your life. It is about becoming alive. It is the Gateway to the Eternal Being in you. It is about becoming who you really are.

Action: Focus on the only thing you have, the present moment.

5.4 Engage Teacher: Engage

But Clint I love, because Clint was my mentor.
I knew nothing about making an Italian movie.
— Eli Wallach

A mentor is someone who sees
more talent and ability within you,
than you see in yourself,
and helps bring it out of you.
— Bob Proctor

Being with a Master is never comfortable, because
He will break all your limitations, all your ideologies.
— Jaggi Vasudev

At Phase III, you are expected to engage Teacher. We
formalized this engagement as a system of personal coaching and
mentoring. This Vortex calls you to go beyond your concerns
about Teacher — and focus your intent onto your deepest self by
engaging Teacher in person.

You enter Phase III (and "graduate from" Phase II) when the
desire for deeper commitment awakens within you. Moving
toward deeper commitment, you will intuitively feel, will bring
more joy and satisfaction to you. An intuition will arise in you —
the intuition that happiness and fulfillment come from having a
deeper purpose and a deeper engagement with your life. Simply
put, you wake up to your life and your wisdom, hidden deep in
your soul.

As you pull closer to your deepest self, a feeling of lightness
and lightheartedness comes to you. Burdens of mind, heavy with
worries and concerns, relax and disperse because of the Love you
feel as you reconnect to It through engaging Teacher, Teachings,
and Work. Your soul begins to shine through — you are happy,
playful, and eager for life. In other words, it all becomes better
and deeper when you personally engage Work, Teaching, and
Teacher.

As a part of his job, Teacher will help you focus your life on more joy and satisfaction by addressing concrete issues that block your way and will work with you on increasing the unblocked energy by encouraging more positive habits.

We packaged your meeting with Teacher as a coaching package of twelve sessions. This is the recommended minimum but you can choose to do more coaching if needed or desired. The minimum of twelve sessions usually gives sufficient time for personal interaction with Teacher at this stage of the process.

If needed, there could be a mentoring component to coaching. Younger people tend to need more mentoring than coaching. If you seek guidance, a system to follow, techniques to practice, Teacher will give you directions, prescribe a routine and follow up on your progress as part of the process of engaging.

Action: Passionately engage in twelve sessions of individual coaching.

5.5 Habits

The hard must become a habit,
the habit must become easy,
the easy beautiful.
— Doug Henning

Our habitual behavior creates a unique inner environment, and influences us just like the external surroundings created by our relatives, friends, colleagues at work, happenings, and events. Our habits, just like external influences, are a type of mind-food on which we feed. And we are what we eat in more than one way!

Our habits (of mind, feelings, and body) and their influence on us are harder to deal with because our habits are frequently unconscious or semi-conscious. They form a part of who we are (or rather who we perceive ourselves to be). In fact, we can define our unique personality as a collection of our unique mental habits. From this point of view, our habits are more problematic than external influences.

Moreover, our habits do have a life of their own. (They have their own authenticity.) That is why it is hard to kick a bad habit. That is why many people who think they are "clear" find out that they are not when stressed enough. The "life" in their habits may spring up at any moment, leaving the victim feeling out of control.

Most people when they become aware of or confronted with a bad habit focus on ridding themselves of the habit. But putting emphasis on the problem, rather than on a solution, does not work. What we resist persists. What we fight against usually increases in our life. Focusing on a habit will make it more important and more prominent.

The best way to deal with bad habits is to work on creating positive habits. If you ignore your bad habits, you stop feeding them! For pesky habits, professional intervention could be a good idea. Teacher as a mentor or coach, for example, can help you focus on creating positive changes in your life, rather than trying to run away from negative habits, which reinforces them. Also, keeping a company of good people is an easy way to get their good habits rub off on you.

Action: Mind influence of your own habits.

5.6 Authenticity

This is a very important practice.
Live your daily life in a way that
you never lose yourself.
When you are carried away with your
worries, fears, cravings, anger, and desire,
you run away from yourself and you lose yourself.
The practice is always to go back to oneself.
— Thich Nhat Hanh

This Vortex asks you — draws you — to be authentic.

You were born with a particular energy, mind, body, emotions. These are gifts given to you, and they are uniquely yours. Being yourself — focusing on and embodying your gifts — opens you up to joy in everyday living, to being happy now, to feeling like hugging everyone in your life. The world responds by showing you the best side of people and things.

By learning to be your authentic self, you tune into your life's purpose and get in touch with the Divine Love that permeates this amazing Universe. You were meant to be this way — your way! The biggest mistake we make is not accepting how God made us — because it is the ultimate rejection of God and Nature, your own nature. The purpose of your life is found in being authentic!

Yet, a common spiritual malady is pretending to be someone else in hopes of being accepted by others. By presenting a false persona we invite acceptance and love toward a mask — a false image we create for the benefit of eliciting a positive response from others. We lie about ourselves because we do not believe deep down we are lovable the way we are.

A false persona is a type of resistance, an energy blockage. Being your authentic self is about letting your energies flow freely. An inauthentic expression always implies an inner resistance of some sort. By being yourself, you release these blocks and begin to experience more vitality, joy, and love that were all yours to begin with. That is why they say it is your birthright!

See the Vortex "Be yourself" for a complementary (negative) view of the topic, on page 66.

Action: Be authentic with respect to yourself and others. Let your energy and your gifts flow through you with gusto and abandon!

5.7 Madhuvidya

Divine Love is distinguished from human love
in this supremely important particular:
it is free from particularity.
— James Allen

The temple bell stops
but I still hear the sound
coming out of the flowers.
— Basho

The path to creating a life worth living — a life of passion,
wisdom and joy — is about synchronizing your personal will with
the Will of God (or call It the Will of Universe, if you must). This
Vortex invites you to experience that fact directly.

Madhuvidya is a subtler version of period intending. Instead
of focusing your intentions on what you want, you begin to tune
your mind to what the Universe wants for you. If the "Period
Intending" Vortex was about your will, this Madhuvidya Vortex is
about God's will. The task here is synchronizing the two wills —
your microcosmic will and the Universal Macrocosmic Will.

Madhuvidya translates as *sweet knowing* (Sanskrit). It is
about tasting sweetness of the Divine Love in every moment of
your life. We live in joy when we realize that life — yours and
mine — is wonderful, that colorful flowers in meadows, lush trees
in forests, and diverse people on streets are sweet because they
are sweet.

This sweet happiness attracts what you want to you. But you
will not care about receiving then — because you wanted
happiness and now you have joy. You thought that happiness
comes from having things — but once you are happy those agents
are not needed.

That is why great Swami Vivekananda said: "Fortune is like a
flirt; she cares not for him who wants her, but she is at the feet of

him who does not care for her. Money comes and showers itself upon one who does not care for it; so does fame come in abundance until it is a trouble and a burden. They always come to the Master. The slave never gets anything. The Master is he who can live in spite of them, whose life does not depend upon the little, foolish things of the world."

In the "Law of Attraction" community, the common belief is that if you visualize what you want you will get it. *"Ask and it is given"*, they say. This is certainly true — if we fancy gross generalizations. However, to receive what you want you need to know what you *truly* want. And knowing what you really want is a challenge — a question of awareness and maturity.

Yet, developing the awareness and maturity enough to activate the Law of Attraction takes special effort. Proper training is required to learn how to activate the Law of Attraction — as, for instance, is presented by Modern Seers Vortexes. Such training is a subtle task, traditionally attempted only under competent supervision, something that authentic Teachers know well. That is why the Vivekananda's quote above comes from his lecture "Sadhanas or Preparations for Higher Life". He knew.

You need to be kind to yourselves if you cannot fathom Madhuvidya right away. Living in joy and Divine Sweetness does not happen immediately. You cannot say to yourself "I shall be happy from now on" when your neighbor is evil, your job insecure, your spouse abusive, and you think you have a weight problem. It is the job of Teacher to communicate to you about the length and effort of the training required. It is your job to hear Teacher's words, stay encouraged, and succeed.

The technique: Ideate that each period is infused with God's love for you and others. Ideate that God is working to give you the best experience, the best learning, the best life possible under the circumstances. Ideate that God is with you. Ideate that God uses you as His instrument for each action that you perform. Relax into His will and experience His sweetness!

If you forget to do the practice before the period starts, do the ideating at the time when you remember.

Action: Draw yourself to the Sweetness of Everything, and enjoy!

5.8 Cosmic brotherhood

> Thousands of candles can be lighted
> from a single candle,
> and the life of the candle will not be shortened.
> Happiness never decreases by being shared.
> — The Buddha

This Vortex encourages you to go beyond narrow thinking for the time has come to embrace one universal family.

This Vortex urges awareness that we are children of Singular Energy. We all came from this Universe. We are brothers and sisters born from the same Mother and Father. Humans, animals, plants, stones, oceans, and rivers — all came from one source. We are one family and should treat each other accordingly.

Narrow thinking tops the list of the world problems we face today. Many people still favor their race (racism), country (nationalism), area (provincialism) at the expense of others. One community (communalism) harbors endemic hate against another community (e.g., anti-Semitism and homophobia). Professionals fleece common folk. People who believe in one religion believe another belief is bad.

We are living in the 21st century for goodness sake! It is way beyond time to quit narrow views and embrace Cosmic Brotherhood. Abandon all unscientific, irrational, sectarian narrow-mindedness. Discard ethnocentric, religiocentric, nationalist, provincial, communal, homophobic thoughts. Rid yourself of hate! Ditch any ideology — however much you might love it — that promotes someone over another. Be part of this Universe Who is fair to all its children. Does it matter how we call our Divine Parents — God, the Force, or the Mind?

How to engage this Vortex: Consider these questions: Does this ideology, belief system, thought habits serve me? Do these thoughts help me or my cosmic brothers and sisters? Ditch useless dogmas from your life!

Embracing Cosmic Brotherhood has nothing to do with abandoning your culture and traditions. Traditions are wonderful, colorful cultural tapestries that make living on our planet a sumptuous feast of diverse fun. Traditions should be cultivated! Yet, it is precisely when traditions are mistaken for sacred or received truth that all hell breaks loose — quite literally at times. Traditions that cultivate views that are against Cosmic Brotherhood must be abandoned with gusto. Replace them with something loving and wholesome.

Action: Love everyone fairly — for all is God's creation.

5.9 Retreats at Phase III: Validation

> Faith is a knowledge within the heart,
> beyond the reach of proof.
> — Khalil Gibran

> It is wrong always, everywhere, and for everyone,
> to believe anything upon insufficient evidence.
> — William Clifford

The retreats intensify the process of transformation — a key objective of Modern Seers. They intensify the training toward reaching for and staying focused on your soul's flow and direction. In addition, the retreats provide a concentrated form of energy — blessings that are much easier to attract and experience with a group of like-minded people than in a social isolation by yourself.

By Phase III, you are now firmly walking your particular path. By now, you have tested the waters enough and have confirmed that this is likely the place that you want to be in (but not beyond all doubt). By this time, you have experienced benefits of attending Modern Seers retreats and other programs: you felt manifestations of Guru Principle during lectures, classes, mentoring and coaching and benefited from that Presence — which we call "direct teaching". And when your peers share, comment, or ask questions, you feel friendly and loving energies that complement each other and increase the presence of Guru Principle. Thus, you have directly experienced and benefited of the "incubator effect" — the power of focused group intention.

At Phase III, you seek to validate your experience, you seek confirmation that the experience is not fleeting. The retreats — advanced or not — are a concentrated, direct way to experience the teaching and receive such validation. You do this before getting into Phase IV when your commitment will become earnest and enduring. Such dedication leads to the experience of much deep-rooted meaning and deep-seated joy in your life. This validation of your experience is a serious affair: note how much time we estimate it will take.

Phase III students are recommended to attend four weekend (short) retreats and two weeklong retreats per a year or more. It is best to schedule attending the retreats evenly, i.e., attend short retreats quarterly and weeklong retreat six months apart or so. Short retreats are 2-3 days long, usually starting Thursday or Friday afternoon till Sunday morning (ends after a brunch). Weeklong retreats last 7-10 days.

Action: Attend four weekend retreats and two weeklong retreats per a year or more.

6 Vortexes for Happy Mind

Happiness is when
what you think, what you say, and what you do
are in harmony.
— Mahatma Gandhi

Too many wish to be happy before becoming wise.
— Suzanne Curchod Necker

6.1 Honor your feelings

Where your treasure is,
there your heart will be also.
— Jesus (Matthew 6:21)

Feelings — both negative or positive — are indications of how things are in your life and where you are going. This Vortex guides you to become aware and respect these indicators.

Feelings are natural — they confirm we are alive. Furthermore, your feelings give indication where you want to go — they point in the direction of happiness. Cut off your feelings, and you will be lost and your life will be dry and colorless.

We feel emotions when there is a friction between the inner and the outer. We experience feelings when our soul — our inner core, the Source or the Divine within us — wants to tell us something. Feeling comfortable or uncomfortable (good or bad) is a communication from our Higher Self. When you think or do something and there is a feeling of discomfort, it is an indication that you are moving away from your inner core. When you engage in any action that moves you in the direction of your life's purpose, you will always feel more pleasant and more at peace than otherwise. Hence, the Joseph Campbell's famous pronouncement: "Follow your bliss".

Let us take another look at this. Feelings tell you where you are in relation to where you want to be. If you have predominantly positive emotions — that is you are generally a happy person — it shows that you are close to where you need to go, to where your life journey is taking you. If you have predominantly negative emotions — that is you are unhappy — that would indicate that you are misaligned, moving away from where you should be in relation to your soul's journey.

Therefore, becoming aware of and respecting your feelings are the key skills to being satisfied in life. Your feelings are the only way to know reliably where you are and where you want to go. No one can tell you better, not even your closest friends or relatives. Feeling are not perfect indicators but they are the only dependable clues we have.

In the past it was common to ignore feelings. Children were told what they should feel and when. Generations of people suppressed their emotions because, due to their ignorance, they focused on survival. However, when we ignore our feelings what they indicate only gets bigger. A small problem becomes a bigger one. And at the extreme, a suppressed emotional condition will manifest as disease. Such manifestations must be heard, for feelings are our soul's messages, or our soul will make them heard.

When you become aware of your feelings, either through a meditation method or by simply being sensitive and mindful, you can "receive" these communications and "process" what these feeling indicate. You can then make an informed decision based on the internal information rather than what external influences dictate.

It is common for people to behave in disrespectful, even violent, ways towards their feelings. They stuff their emotions forcefully under the carpet of their everyday consciousness, in order to appear more composed than they really are. But emotions are energies, and they should not be stuffed into a bottle and let go into a sea for some hapless mariner to release the genie. Eventually, such movement away from wellbeing will manifest as discontent or even physical disease. Meditation is a good cure for the problem of stuffed emotions.

Honoring your feelings is also about making your feelings flow naturally. If you are feeling something, you are. There is no need to pretend that you are feeling something else or not feeling the feeling at all. Let other know how you feel in calm, respectful, and culturally-appropriate ways.

Action: Listen to and honor your feelings.

6.2 Generosity

> Giving is an essential for spiritual unfoldment,
> for until we give and give abundantly,
> we don't really realize that we are not the giver;
> we are just a channel for giving.
> — Sivaya Subramuniyaswami

Be generous! You are a mysterious traveler on the Path, just like everyone else. When you give, you open yourself up to receiving.

Generosity has two functions: a social function and a deeper, spiritual function. We are all together on this path of life: being generous makes things smooth, creates friends, and makes you look good in front of others.

But generosity is also an indication that you are secure in your abundance; you know that the universe is a safe and bountiful place for you. A generous person broadcasts to the Source that he or she is aware of the Divine eternal abundance and, thus, opens him- or herself to new possibilities, which common folk call miracles. A truly generous person attracts good things to him or herself. Authentic generosity calls forth a life that is abundantly rich with experiences and fun people and things to play with.

The best way to understand how generosity is a key component to emotional wellbeing is that generosity is an indication of how open you are to life. It's an indication of a "valve" you have inside; a valve that takes amazing things from life, and lets them pass through you to be released onto others.

When you are open and you are being generous, two things happen. Firstly, it allows you to let go of things that do not need to be stuck with you. It's a way to use things in your life, rather than horde them. It also allows for new things to come into your life. If you are not generous it will be difficult for you to open the door for new things, new events, and new people to enter.

Therefore, generosity is by far the best way how you can have a rich life, and not just financially. If you are tight-fisted, your "vibration" is not of someone who will attract money into his or her life. Tight-fisted people suffer from poverty mentality, a scarcity of the spirit. Even though, you may drive a very expensive car, it will not make you *feel* rich. You don't need anything material to feel abundant. Generously giving what you do not need clears the space for new things and events to come to your life.

Generosity can be (and should be) cultivated but it must never be forced. We can cultivate generosity by becoming aware of fear that manifests as possessiveness and greed. A greedy person feels "this is mine — I own this" and makes his fist tight, her body constricted. Letting the energy flow is better! We are extensions of One Universal Mind, emanations of One Source, and are taken care of by the Universe, if we let It do Its job.

(Any legislative redistribution of wealth is an expression of scarcity mentality. A society definitely needs to regulate property rights. Vibrant spiritual life is the way to bring real prosperity into society.)

Let us say a few words about neurotic generosity, the tendency to be generous in order to please others. In other words, not being authentically generous but playing a generosity game. Playing this make-belief is common in the "create-your-own-reality" community where people pretend to be generous in order to attract wealth. The authentic desire here is to become financially rich, not be abundant. These people try to become prosperous through manipulation. This is- "How can I manipulate God in order to get what I want?", rather than "How can I open myself up to God so that I will not want much besides God?" All God hears is what a manipulative schemer you are...

If a person is identified with his or her ego and is possessive, he or she should not be "forced" to be generous (by inducing guilt, for instance). If a person realizes his or her possessiveness and wants to go beyond his or her greediness by cultivating generosity, then the task can be accomplished by him– or herself or by engaging a Teacher (guru) who will engage you, force the issue, and train you to be generous.

Action: Attract abundance to yourself by being generous.

6.3 Admit your mistakes

A man must be big enough to admit his mistakes,
smart enough to profit from them,
and strong enough to correct them.
— John C. Maxwell

Mistakes are a fact of life.
It is the response to error that counts.
— Nikki Giovanni

You engage this Vortex every time you choose to be honest about your mistakes with yourself and others. To err is human, but to come clean divine. Admitting mistakes is about going forward.

When you acknowledge your mistakes, it is about moving on, rather than being stuck. It helps diffuse negative or confusing feelings before they swell out of control. It shows that you don't have a need to be always right.

Admitting your mistakes is good for you. Mistakes that you do not fess up to fester within you, creating tension. Sooner or later, you will project this internal conflict onto others, usually in passive-aggressive ways. Or blame others for your mistake.

If you don't address a mistake promptly your conscience will keep replaying the memory of the "crime scene". You will "meditate" on your mistake in your mind, and its smarting emotions will create an expanded vision of it. The distortion introduced by the mistake will grow in your mind. Do you really wish to summon that kind of reality to yourself?

Admitting your mistakes is about being transparent with yourself and others. Being frank with yourself about your behavior and not lying to others about your faults keeps your mind free from clutter. It takes a lot of energy to be in denial — or to juggle multiple stories in your head, trying to remember what story you told to whom.

A true admission of mistake involves having a sincere remorse and a desire to correct the mistake committed. Admitting your mistake to yourself and to others — if needed — is a big part of making amends. Forgiving yourself for making the mistake is essential for moving forward and beyond.

Dealing with mistakes effectively is about working with the shadow, the hidden part of our psyche that contains our repressed shortcomings and instincts. The encounter with the shadow plays a central part in individuation, the process of integration through which a person becomes his or her true self.

The less we are aware of the shadow, the more it will reveal itself in dysfunctional ways. The shadow is irrational — it likes turning a personal inferiority into a deficiency in someone else.

The shadow can be discovered and understood but is difficult to get rid of. Thus, working on your shadow is a daily chore and a life-long process. Being open about one's faults is evidence of shadow under control.

In youth, we make many mistakes — as an integral part of growing up. Having a mentor, someone who you truly respect and admire, provides a person to whom you can openly lay your cards out and allow them to straighten you out. The intimacy with your mentor wherein you are willing to admit your deepest shadow material — admit to him or her what is hard to admit even to yourself — is a great privilege because it is so incredibly rare.

Confessing your wrong doings to your mentor quickly removes the guilt felt by young person and provides much needed relief to go beyond the mistake, continue with life, and thrive. Besides by not letting the energy of a mistake fester, a mentor can offer a fresh perspective on the mistake — something we crave much in youth — in search of our own experience with life.

Saving face and admitting your mistakes are not in conflict with one another. Admitting your mistake shows your superior spiritual quality. Indeed, you are saving your face when you do not hide your mistakes. You present yourself as a good person willing to be part of the group.

On the deepest level, mistakes are just lessons to learn, the mind to be expanded, new perspectives to be gained. There is no shame in making mistakes. We are all humans living with a limited perspective in some way.

When you admit your mistakes and move on, you get an opportunity to focus on the new, on the future, on what you want, rather than endlessly repeating the energy from grievances from the past mistake.

Action: Admit your mistakes and move forward.

6.4 Forgiveness

A wise man will make haste to forgive,
because he knows the true value of time,
and will not suffer it to pass away in unnecessary pain.
— Samuel Johnson

To forgive is the highest,
Most beautiful form of love.
In return you will receive
Untold peace and happiness.
— Robert Muller

Forgiveness frees you from grievances against others, big or small. This Vortex calls you to forgive those who wronged you and free yourself!

Forgiveness is a decision to let go of resentment and thoughts of revenge. Forgiveness brings peace and restores joy to your life. Forgiveness doesn't justify the wrong committed against you. Forgiveness is not about reconciling with the person that hurt you, or condoning their actions. You can forgive without excusing the person or action that hurt you.

If you hold on to resentments, you will inject anger and bitterness into every new experience and relationship. Your life may become so focused on the wrongs others committed against you that you will weaken the connection to your soul (your Source). As the result, you will not be able to fully enjoy the present, staying stuck in the past. Forgiveness brings back meaning and purpose to your life because it unblocks you and reconnects you back to your Source, the source of joy and meaning.

Forgiveness is about changing the story you keep on telling yourself about who and what hurt you. Once your recognize the value of forgiveness you can examine how you developed the negative habit, and this reflection will begin to move you from feeling a victim to taking back control of and restoring joy and peace in your life.

It is natural to dislike someone who wronged you. The world is full of people who hurt us — on purpose, by accident, or via their incompetence. The emotion of dislike could be beneficial if it opens a new perspective into yourself and others and serves as a way to expand your mind. But you may get attached to these emotions. The severity and duration of this attachment depend on the density of your ego. (Spiritual practices such as these Vortexes reduce the density of your ego, making it lighter.)

If the attachment to these grievances is severe, forgiveness may be difficult. Some people live their entire lives bearing grudges against relatives, friends, entire nations, or groups of people. The way out of this predicament is acknowledging these grievances openly (and publicly, if appropriate) and then moving on by letting go of them. By accepting your current state, you can recognize it and then let go of it — gradually or faster. Don't let your small grievances become so large that you hate the entire group to which the man or woman who wronged you belongs to.

But the greatest problem with holding any grievance is that it injects its vibration into our consciousness, just like any other thought. When we feel anger toward someone or something we create a negative feeling within us, which if consistent, will continually generate the bad thoughtform within us. If you want to live in happiness, you want to avoid creating preconditions for unhappy manifestations in your life. You want to move on from hurt and anger to a different — positive — stream of consciousness that exudes a vibration of contentment and joy.

Forgiveness feels like drinking from a cool spring after many months in a hot desert. It is relieving and freeing — and opens you up to peace and joy. Forgiveness is about you becoming free.

Action: Forgive and be free!

6.5 Beauty

When I admire the wonder of a sunset
or the beauty of the moon,
my soul expands in worship of the creator.
— Mahatma Gandhi

I can't stop pointing to the beauty.
Every moment and place says,
"Put this design in your carpet!"
— Jalaluddin Rumi

Take notice of the beauty around you, and you will engage this Vortex. Beauty makes your mind and heart sing with delight.

Working on your connection with God begins with appreciating beauty. When we connect to the Source — "the Higher Power" — the "state" manifests as joy. Beauty is how we open ourselves to spiritual path.

Seeking and appreciating beautiful things makes us notice that the world has many facets, toward which we were blind before. Appreciating beautiful things refines our egos and opens us to the mystery of the Source (God).

Beauty is one "level" above the intellect, the place where we tend to be stuck as humanity. Humanity today is obsessed with the rational more than ever before, still trying to keep a lid on the transrational ever leaking in.

Science is about studying the world using logic to understand cause and effect and developing new beneficial tools through the rational approach. Art is about seeking finer ways — cultivating subtler styles, acquiring deeper perceptions, and developing delicate conceptional nuances. Appreciating art is a step up beyond the intellect toward the transrational.

Modern humans are smart in the usual sense but they are not wise — because their intuitive knowing is underdeveloped. Someone who acquired much intellectual wealth — an educated person — may be so stuck in the "brain" that he or she cannot appreciate other perspectives. Appreciating finer things refines the mind and makes it aware of wisdom, the byproduct of intuitive knowing. Without attaining wisdom, lasting contentment and happiness are impossible — there are no ifs and buts about it.

A person who appreciates beauty moves quicker toward finer perceptions — beyond the limits of the senses and intellect, toward intuitive knowing, the abode of wisdom.

To be sure, beauty is in the eye of the beholder. This is true to a point, though. What you consider beautiful today may change through cultivation, education, and experience. What beauty you see and where you find it is as much about personal preference as about fostering and developing your finer faculties. You may enjoy classical music today and savor jazz ten years down the line. You may or may not find beauty in the scorched desert shrubs. You may find beauty in a perfectly manicured lawn or a messy but functional office of a dear friend.

Avoid worrying about what is and is not beautiful for you. This question is for another discussion. Instead, go and find inspiration in the beauty that is beautiful for you. Behold colorful flowers, observe attractive people, pet graceful cats, recite delightful poetry, listen to sumptuous music. In other words, savor the beauty that inspires you!

There are two ways to seek out beauty. You can train yourself to see beauty around you in everything but this may be hard at the beginning. Or you can take a gradual approach. You can engage in creative pursuits such as writing, painting, and music. Regular visits to an art museum or gallery are another option. The soul sees life, light, and beauty everywhere. Only the judging mind sees ugliness. You can gradually make your soul the dominant seer of beauty in your life.

Action: Surround yourself with beautiful things for inspiration.

6.6 Healthy food

The best six doctors anywhere
And no one can deny it
Are sunshine, water, rest, and air
Exercise and diet.
These six will gladly you attend
If only you are willing
Your mind they'll ease
Your will they'll mend
And charge you not a shilling.
— Nursery rhyme

Eating good food is good for your mood! Such declaration should not surprise anyone, particularly if you are interested in developing intuition and wisdom. This Vortex calls you to become aware how food you eat influences your mind and emotions.

You will do well if you follow the "Good food" Vortex (see page 115) and other Modern Seers teachings on nutrition. Still, a few points deserve a special mention.

Good food naturally improves your mood, ability to concentrate, and energy level. Fresh fruit and vegetables give you more energy. You become more physically active as your energy level increases. The additional exercise increases pleasure chemicals in the brain and is a natural mood elevator.

Lighter food makes emotional energy flow better than heavier foods. Proper food combining is also conducive to higher and smoother moods and making emotions flow and release better. Bad food combinations and heavy foods tend to make emotions heavy and stuck. Therefore, eat a balanced diet with less carbs and proteins and more fresh veggies and fruits.

Some stress is great for spiritual growth and mental expansion but suffering prolonged stress depletes natural sedatives, stimulants, and pain relievers in the body. Avoid such adverse circumstances.

Do not use addictive foods such as refined sugars and flours as those inhibit the production of natural pleasure chemicals in the brain. Refined sugars such as regular table white sugar and high-fructose corn syrup should be strictly avoided. Same goes for white refined wheat flour, which rules out eating most commercially baked product. Yes, read the ingredients label! Refined (milled) rice is only slightly less bad and should be avoided as well.

Most people eat too much carbs and too little quality protein. Your brain relies on quality protein — the only food source for amino acids — to make all of its natural mood-elevating substances.

Most people's nutrition is deficient in Omega-3 fatty acids, important substances for happy mood. Milk from grass fed cattle is the only good non-plant source of these essential nutrients.

Good food creates good vibrations and makes you feel better. Enjoy lighter food if you want to stay in a good mood.

Action: Eat good food for a vibrant mind!

7 Vortexes for Healthy Body

A healthy body is a guest-chamber for the soul;
a sick body is a prison.
— Francis Bacon

The groundwork of all happiness is health.
— James Leigh Hunt

The Phase I students should follow these as guidelines.
The Phase II students should attempt to become strict.
The Phase III students should follow these without a compromise.

If due to your health circumstances a health care professional
recommends against any suggestions found in this section,
do follow his or her advice.

7.1 Honor your body

Take care of your body.
It's the only place you have to live.
— Jim Rohn

Your body is a temple, but only if you treat it as one.
— Astrid Alauda

Your body is the temple where you live. This Vortex calls you to honor this temple — to open up to and embrace body's natural capacity to heal and live in joy.

We honor our body by listening to it when it needs attention and letting it be when it does not. Your body communicates. These messages can be quiet, loud, or in between. Waiting for the body to shout: "Don't ignore me!" is going too far. Hearing the messages when they are still subtle is probably the best.

Most of us have lost some or most of the capacity to receive messages from our body. Parents, schools, culture, food industry, and curative ideologies of the day typically damage our natural relationship with the body early on. Most of us must re-train ourselves to have a functional relationship with our physical temples. Hence, this Vortex.

Human body has natural cycles — its own authentic rhythm. It knows well what it needs and when: when to eat, what to eat, when to sleep or wake up, and how to heal. As best as you can, you should not disrupt this natural functioning of your body.

Yet, we train from early on to break these cycles. We subject our body to discipline in youth and struggle to relax the discipline later on. In the name of social convention, we force our children up at dawn for school. Yet, letting the young sleep in improves their learning abilities. We force our kids to eat food they dislike because we believe it is good for them. We suppress our natural urge to go potty because we are in a business meeting.

We have "civilized" our body to the point it almost forgot its natural needs and cycles. Should we act surprised when the body becomes dysfunctional — and gets unwell?

If you are in tune with your body, it will tell you what it needs to stay healthy and balanced. For a perceptive person it is common to walk around a market and feel drawn to get particular fruits or vegetables.

People who pursue deeper awareness spend considerable time remembering the connection they have with their body, inviting the body to give them information for moving toward, while staying in wellness. The body is a shrine wherein Sacred Divine lives — we should treat it accordingly.

Action: Honor your body and be natural about your body's needs.

7.2 Meditation for healing

> Within my body are
> all the sacred places of the world,
> and the most profound pilgrimage I can ever make
> is within my own body.
> — Saraha

> There is more wisdom in your body than
> in your deepest philosophy.
> — Friedrich Nietzsche

Meditation practice is by far the best catalyst for physical well-being and for healing the body and keeping it healthy. This Vortex pulls you into this awareness.

A meditation practice encourages health and healing through superior listening to your body. The body will heal itself if you allow it to return to its natural cycles, do not stress it unnecessarily, and feed it nutrition it naturally desires. But you need to tune yourself to your body's communication to you.

Meditation works on many levels for healing the body. Primarily it promotes less stress and more deep relaxation as well as recognition and alleviation of dysfunctional behaviors, including your relationship to food and work. In the modern information-intensive world, meditation practice helps clear away the information overload that builds up every day and contributes to your stress.

The influence of meditation practice on health, emotions, and physiology has been widely researched and discussed in research publications. Current research confirms what the East has known for centuries: Meditation has positive influence on health. It has been confirmed to increase happiness by resolving negative thinking and increasing positive emotion, alleviate anxiety and depression, boost the immune system, lower blood pressure, and lower blood sugar. Meditation also helps with overeating — you will recognize better when you are about to overeat and have an opportunity to choose a better alternative. Meditation is also useful if you have a health condition that may be worsened by stress.

Almost all problems that can be solved with increased awareness. If you meditate regularly, you will tend to choose fresher air to breathe, more frequent baths to keep your body clean and cool, more balanced meals that do not clog your system up, and a less stressful lifestyle. If you go to work with meditative approach in mind you will overwork less but be more productive with your time — by noticing better when you are wasting your time being nonproductive. If you walk into grocery market in a meditative state, you will naturally choose foods that are better suited to your body and its wellbeing. At each point of your life, you will make better choices for your health and well-being — if you are a regular meditator.

Action: Meditate to listen better to your body for health and wellbeing.

7.3 Drink lots of liquid

> I distrust camels, and anyone else
> who can go a week without a drink.
> — Joe E. Lewis

> I never drink water.
> I'm afraid it will become habit-forming.
> — W. C. Fields

> I drink a gallon of water a day.
> — Gabrielle Union

Drink plenty of water, juices, teas per day. Become a lemon water fanatic. "Good hydration" is the mantra for this Vortex.

Our body consists mostly of water. Water is the conduit and lubricant, the substance that keeps things afloat and moving in the body. Thus, we must keep the body well hydrated in order for it to function properly.

If the body does not have enough water, it cannot effectively receive and absorb nutrients and then expel the unusable waste. Thus, if we want to have a healthy body, we must drink plenty of fluids (and eat good food). So, drink a good amount of water, teas, and juices!

Water has different properties depending on the source. Leaving the discussion on good practices for the planet's ecology, tap water is not good because it has a stagnant "vibration" after all the processing it must undergo to make it "fit" for human consumption. Distilled water, although it is chemically pure, is also dead. The best water naturally flows from an artesian well or a spring.

You can make tap water or distilled water a bit more alive by placing it in a clear glass jar with one or two cabbage leaves. If you use tap water, you should filter it first. Place the jar on a windowsill in the direct sun light for several hours. Cabbage will draw most of the toxins out, including bad vibrations, and the sun will infuse living force (prana) into the water. We tested this method with a few other vegetables — and cabbage seems to work best.

It is better to drink liquids between meals, half an hour before and two-three hours after eating, the timing depends on the type and size of the meal. During meals, beverages should be consumed sparingly as they tend to dilute the gastric juices, getting in the way of digestion. Drink the bulk of water in the morning, as the body is dehydrated at the night.

If your body is dehydrated such as after being in the sun, sauna, or airplane, then it is better to drink water with some grape or apple juice in a ratio of 3 or 4 to 1. This is similar to commercial sports drinks but without all the artificial colors and preservatives. If you have access to coconut water, it is probably the best drink to re-hydrate yourself.

Caffeinated drinks such as regular tea, coffee, non-decaffeinated green tea are stimulants and make you lose water. Ingesting caffeine is not recommended if you wish to build strong spiritual energy in meditation.

Lemon water helps good digestion and elimination. To prepare, squeeze half a lemon in a glass of water and add a pinch of salt. (Lime or Indian lemon can also be used — use the whole one if small.) Lemon stimulates the liver, and salt helps move food matter through the intestines. Lemon water is particularly good in the morning, if you have difficulty with elimination (i.e., if you have a tendency toward constipation).

During the day, it is better to drink lemon water with a bit of honey, instead of salt. We have been also experimenting with liquid stevia extracts to add calorie-free flavors to lemon water; try chocolate raspberry flavor, for example.

If you have a cold or a flu and you need to cleanse the body, use maple syrup instead of honey and add a pinch of cayenne pepper to the drink. This is called "master cleanser" drink.

Some authorities say that a gallon (about 4 liters) of liquids should be consumed per day to keep the body optimally healthy. This is, of course, in addition to having a clean and healthy diet, which is supported by the next "Good food" Vortex.

Action: Drink plenty of liquids.

7.4 Good food

Animals feed, people eat;
but only the intelligent people know how to eat.
— Anthelme Brillat-Savarin

Those who think they have no time for healthy eating
will sooner or later have to find time for illness.
— Edward Stanley

You enter this Vortex when you pay attention to food you eat. As the famous quote goes, "tell me what you eat and I shall tell you what you are." (The phrase first appeared in *Physiology of Taste, or Meditations on Transcendental Gastronomy*, the book published in 1826 by French doctor and gourmand, Anthelme Brillat-Savarin.)

Being oblivious about food we eat is appallingly common. This is true even with all the constant media attention to healthy eating and research by nutrition professionals. But such ignorance is unwise because food does matter for our health, mood, and speed of spiritual evolution.

Food has two qualities that we should always consider: nutritional and vibrational. We usually ignore the latter. Living food makes you more alive. Soothing food calms you down. Stimulating food makes you more active. Food that makes life energy (prana or qi) flow better brings about a more relaxed and perceptive you. A cow freely grazing at a lush green meadow will give milk full of love. The integrity of the growers behind the wheat in your bread will influence both your health and your spiritual progress.

What is the best food to eat? We recommend that you increase raw fruits and vegetables in your diet. A raw vegetarian (vegan) diet retains life force (prana or qi) and enzymes that are commonly destroyed when you heat-treat the foods.

Properly combining food types in your means is equally important. Meals that are poorly combined pollute your body with partially digested food. Different environments in the stomach are necessary for digesting various types of food. For instance, proteins require acid environment but carbohydrates need more of an alkaline environment. Thus, a standard meal in most regions of the world — protein (e.g., meat or beans) and carbs (e.g., potatoes or white rice) — is a bad combination because the acid-alkaline conflict will prevent good digestion of either. (The standard meals also do not include enough green vegetables, which are important for healing the body.)

Here are a few simple ideas on food combining: Fruits should be eaten separately, about an hour before or three-to-four hours after a meal. Green vegetables can be eaten either with proteins or with carbohydrates — but avoid mixing proteins and carbohydrates as mentioned above. For example, you can eat cabbage with tempeh or cabbage with potatoes but not tempeh and potatoes. Some foods combine well with anything. For example, citrus fruits and pineapple can be included in any meal.

Excessive consumption of protein, starch, and sugar is a worldwide problem. In the West, people consume too much protein — meat and milk. In Asia, people eat too much starch — white rice and potatoes. Overeating and emotional eating is also a problem — both overload our bodies. It is hard to overload your system while eating or snacking on raw vegetables or fruit.

Organic food is preferable. Organic vegetables and fruits are more alive and that life force will benefit your health and mood. Organic produce has less chemical additives such as pesticides and fertilizers that impair the immune system, cause allergies and disease. In addition, organic farming is easier on the environment.

It is good if you prepare your own meals. Your own vibration will not harm you because you are always attuned to yourself, whatever your "level". Furthermore, you can usually increase beneficial qualities of the food by being mindful — meditating or chanting during preparation. When you eat food prepared by another person, his or her mental state will vibrationally "infect" you. Every time you eat out at a café or restaurant, vibrations the owners and the chef will come to your table with the meal and enter your body. Thus, if you eat out, make sure you have positive regard toward the company, the chef, and the waiter.

At Phase I, you can safely ignore this Vortex, even though becoming aware of the good diet would be helpful. At Phase II, you should learn about the benefits of organic food and proper food combining. At Phase III, you should eat predominantly organic food and avoid foods that make you feel dull.

To conclude, you can ignore all the above advice when you become adequately tuned to your body. The more aware you are of your body's needs, the wiser you shall be about the food you eat and its effect on you. This awareness naturally engages this Vortex.

Action: Eat well-combined, organic meals.

7.5 Exercise

A man's health can be judged by which
he takes two at a time — pills or stairs.
— Joan Welsh

After dinner, rest awhile, after supper, walk a mile.
— English saying

This Vortex encourages participation in regular exercise or sport.

Physical exercise such as physical work and exercise is good for health and wellness, as most everyone knows. Physical activity strengthens muscles and the heart, improves immunity to sickness, helps maintain a healthy weight, and is fun. Hiking, swimming, volleyball, soccer, boxing, wrestling, and so on — all are good ways to move and relax the body. The type of exercise you should do depends what you enjoy, of course.

Having light and clean body is crucial when you are seeking to increase your sensitivity to subtle changes, signs, or events and to expand your awareness. Moving your body, exercise, keeps things flowing in the body and helps moving toxins out of the body. That is why exercise is a mood elevator — you feel better and experience more joy after physical activity.

Thus, it is a good idea to engage in moderate exercise every day and a more vigorous physical activity 3-5 times a week. For example, a walk every day or daily asana (yoga) practice will work well for most people. Then, a few times a week you can do something more intensive.

In asana practice, poses and movements help bring energy to the body, calmness to the senses, and stability to the mind. In contrast, conventional exercise routines require repeated and fast, forceful movements. In asana practice, the mind is soothed and senses are quieted down, bringing a state of well-being, a balance between physical and mental aspects.

In the practice of yoga asanas, strength and power development is but one aim. The other — more important — objective is achieving a balance and harmony between your mind, body, emotions, and your inner self (spirit). Other forms of exercise are not holistic because they tend to deal with each particular part of the body separately. After an asana session, you feel joy and rejuvenation. After regular exercise, one feels tired because the activity exhausts the cells and glands, even though conventional exercising does improve the mood and overall energy level.

Best to do your physical activity in the clean, well-ventilated indoors or in fresh air outdoors. When you exercise make sure your heart rate goes up and stays up for a while, good for moving stuff around in the body — and out, if necessary.

Action: Do physical activity regularly.

7.6 Keep clean!

> Bathe twice a day to be really clean,
> once a day to be passably clean,
> once a week to avoid being a public menace.
> — Anthony Burgess

This Vortex reminds you to keep your body and its surroundings clean. Everyone should be aware by now that good hygiene is good for your health. Even though this Vortex should not require much elaboration, let's consider a few thoughts.

First, let us look at a few suggestions that should be common knowledge. Harmful microorganisms and substance are removed by proper washing. Thus, you should wash hands frequently, take a bath or shower daily (or more if needed), shampoo hair regularly. If you believe you came in contact with a contaminated object clean yourself as soon as you can.

Use only natural products in personal care. The skin is the largest organ of the body (by area) and will absorb whatever chemicals you put on it. Use only natural soaps, cosmetics, deodorants, and toothpaste, with herbal ingredients without artificial color or perfume. Most commercial products available through common retail channels are not natural, bad for you, and should be avoided.

Harmful vibrations pollute the body as well. People on the Path are particularly sensitive to bad vibrations. Compromised vibrational quality of food, drink, the environment, clothing, etc. are probably worse for your health than coming in contact with ordinary dirt. But few people notice or pay attention to this fact — even when they are clearly suffering from exposure to such objects. For example, living in a neighborhood with many angry people due to class, ethnic, or other tensions will adversely affect you — it can affect quality of your sleep and digestion, or even cause dryness of your skin. Eating food prepared by a good person, moving to an apartment owned by an honest landlord, never wearing pre-owned clothing close to your skin, etc. can improve your well-being.

Frequent washing also helps remove bad vibrations from affecting your body. If you were in a bad spot and got infected with negative energy, a long shower may help relieve you of the vibrational contamination. If bathing is not possible, washing the affected areas with ample amounts of flowing water will usually reduce the discomfort. (Don't use hot water.)

It is a good idea to use fresh underwear daily — it is good for keeping body vibes high. So change socks, etc. daily. Don't use the smell test. If you wore it for one day, wash it.

The best time for daily bath or shower is in the morning before doing anything else. Water helps remove static vibrations of sleep and freshen you up. You should take more than one bath if the weather is hot, or you need to freshen yourself up.

Treat your body as a temple — do your best to let in only thoughts and vibrations that are worthy of God in and keep the rest out. Treat your home as a temple as well — think of it as an additional item of vibrational hygiene. Do not bring bad thoughts from the outside into your home. Do not wear shoes you use outdoor in your home — not only it is unhygienic, it also brings "vibes" from the outside. Keep your body and home worthy of the Divine, and She will regularly visit you.

Inner hygiene is also about ingesting pure food and beverages, see the "Good food" Vortex (on page 115) for more details.

Action: Keep it clean for good health.

8 Uplift the World Vortexes

How wonderful it is that nobody need wait a single moment
before starting to improve the world.
— Anne Frank

A joyful heart is the inevitable result of a heart burning with love.
— Mother Teresa

8.1 Respect and appreciate

> I always prefer to believe the best of everybody,
> it saves so much trouble.
> — Rudyard Kipling

> To love is to release God's storehouse of golden treasure.
> If we love we cannot help giving,
> and to give is to gain,
> and the law of love is fulfilled.
> — Baird Spalding

The Universe turns its friendly face to those who are nice. You engage this Vortex when you realize that. Treating others with kindness tends to invoke reciprocal behavior, contributing to a nicer environment around you. People instinctively return friendly behavior if you are considerate and pleasant to them.

Being friendly is a step toward loving kindness, a form of devotion. When you meet someone, you are meeting Cosmic Consciousness (the Source) in physical form. Thus, this Vortex is about the quality of attention you direct toward the Divine Being Who is present in everything.

Being nice toward others improves your vibrational quality. All beings know instinctively that a superior vibrational energy brings nicer things to them. We naturally want to increase happiness and well-being in our life. Humans are special because they can consciously engage the process.

To really start pulling what you want from the Universe you need to manifest the space of respect and appreciation — beyond being merely nice and friendly. Respect and appreciation has to be real for this to work. You cannot do the "fake until you make it" bit on this. Real transformation is required. Love and appreciation must become your nature.

Start with being nice and friendly, progress to feeling inspired by every creature and every meeting, engage respect, and let appreciation for God's perfection to come to you. You will know that you are truly engaging this Vortex when being merely nice (sweet and smiling) feels primitive to you.

It is unlikely that you will be able to sustain the feeling of respect and appreciation all the time. Simply downgrade to acting nice and friendly whenever you "slip" from respect and appreciation.

Here are a few thoughts on common challenges on the spiritual path:

- Allow others to be as they are. Asking people to change without their invitation implicitly invalidates them. Do not begrudge people who are not on the same path, do not share the same teacher, or are not in the same vibrational space as you.

- You do not know all the reasons why things are the way they are. Do not criticize people, country, religion, gender, politics, etc. Be respectful — and open to the unknown.

- Being grateful benefits you more than the other party. Acknowledge and appreciate when someone has done something for you. Say thank you even when the other person does not deserve it.

- Be sincere with your hospitality. When you invite someone to your home, welcome the new energy into your life and treat it as God.

- Anything sensually strong can distract or even hurt sensitive people, and spiritual seekers are overwhelmingly sensitive. Avoid wearing distracting, inappropriate, or culturally insensitive clothing. Avoid strong or artificial soap and perfumes. Same goes for body or breath odor.

- Respect personal boundaries and privacy. Be careful with gossiping. Talking behind someone's back without a constructive purpose is likely an expression of self-righteousness or passive-aggressive behavior aimed at isolating or harming another.

- Wasting time of others is disrespectful. The misguided notion that being casual is being carefree and, therefore, spiritual is self-centered and immature.

- Admit your mistakes.

Engaging this Vortex is about remembering to love. This simply means bringing out the natural loving quality of your innermost self. Everyone is loving at their core — all you need to access this "container" of love is to remember that it is "built-in". It is there for you always.

Your thoughts, mood, and behavior set the tone for your entire life. When you treat others with kindness, the same will offered back to you.

Action: Respect and appreciate. If not possible, be friendly and kind.

8.2 Invite up

> Problems are best solved by transcending them
> and looking at them from a higher viewpoint.
> At the higher level,
> the problems automatically resolve themselves
> because of that shift in point of view,
> or one might see there was no problem at all.
> — David R. Hawkins

This Vortex comes into play when you realize that the only way to uplift people out of their misery is by inviting them to come up to the level of thinking where there exists a solution to their problem.

Engaging this Vortex is straightforward — once you let go of a common belief that, in order to help someone, you must descend to their level of thinking and commiserate with them. It is natural to feel empathy when we see someone suffering. But, we frequently lose ourselves in the feeling. In our wish to help, we synchronize our thinking to their problem to the point that we make their problem a part of our mind. As a consequence, we lose our way to a solution.

Say you have a friend involved in an unhappy relationship. You can sympathize with him and let him complain for hours about his love object. The more you listen, the more you will think about his problem. The more your own thoughts resonate with his problem, the more you will think like your friend. As you essentially meditate on his problem, "being with him in his time of pain", you unwittingly become a part of the problem. This doesn't help your friend, and it doesn't help you. Have you ever noticed how draining this commiseration business is?

A functional way of helping your friend would be to distract him away from his thinking about the problem and redirect the conversation toward finding a solution. Thinking about solutions will uplift him out of the "meditation on the problem" mindset into the "meditation on the solution" mindset.

Anyone's usual level of thinking is a vibrational addiction. By the law of resonance, they shall seek out to perpetuate their current vibration, whether consciously or not. It takes effort to change, shift vibration.

The person you are trying to help must see that they are perpetuating their current situation — by indulging into it. You need to make them realize they are stuck in their rut — addicted to their current vibration, their current situation. If they truly intend to change, the Universe (Source or God) will arrange help for them. As Jesus said (Luke 11:9), "Ask and it will be given to you, seek and you will find, knock and the door will be opened to you."

A change in perspective is required for "raising vibration". Your current worldview is born of your current vibration. The world appears differently to you, depending on the color of glasses you wear. Your worldview is the glasses. If you want to work for the solution of the problem, you have to choose a better perspective, higher point of view. You have to change your glasses to change your vibration.

A person you're trying to help must want to be helped. If he or she doesn't want change, don't try to force it. If you press on, they will try to engage you in their world and their vibration — they will try to hook you with their misery and force you to meditate on their trouble.

When helping others, do not descend to the vibrational level of the person or group you're trying to help. Instead, invite people up. Inner transformation is the only way to real change for the better — in individuals and in the society. Thus, people who want change must be vibrational activists.

Action: Invite up — become a vibrational activist!

8.3 Use resources wisely

> The frog does not drink up
> the pond in which he lives.
> — Native American Proverb

This planet Earth is your home. Everyone and everything is valuable on Earth. You engage this Vortex when you realize this.

Our planet is a vibrant, living ecosystem. It does not require an elevated consciousness to understand this. We live in an interdependent relationship with animals and plants, with land, oceans and air. Sane people do not squander their resources. Sane people respect those they depend on. Sane people take care of their home — they use what they got wisely.

You are engaging this Vortex any time you treat our collective resources with care and respect. It does not matter how most humans lost their connection to the home and its inhabitants — through economic hardship, indifference, or obliviousness. This Vortex is about rekindling our connection to our home.

Resources that are available to us are not limited to material or physical assets. Besides their utility value to humans, animals, plants, oceans have value by their existence alone. Human beings have enormous intellectual resources as well as emotional and spiritual assets. All resources should be treated as important — prioritizing in the most efficient way.

Keep in mind the following:

- Develop yourself spiritually as this is the best way to gain wisdom and make decisions from a wise perspective.

- Use your best qualities — the more unique skill or knowledge you have, the more they should be used. High-skilled people should work at jobs where their knowledge is appreciated and used.

- Conserve energy. Live in energy efficient housing. Use efficient vehicles and appliances. Turn the lights off when not in use.

- Conserve fresh water.

- Recycle and support sustainable development.

Do your part at being a conscious inhabitant of this Planet. Use everything and everyone to their highest potential. As we expand our minds through spiritual practices (such as these Vortexes), we will naturally gravitate toward wise use of our resources.

Action: Work on your wisdom to know how to use resources wisely.

8.4 Support conscious business

> When we quit thinking primarily about
> ourselves and our own self-preservation,
> we undergo a truly heroic
> transformation of consciousness.
> — Joseph Campbell

> Be the change you want to see in the world.
> — Mahatma Gandhi

A conscious business is one that respects nature, uses resources wisely, treats people well, and is engaged in business in a way of service. Even though conscious businesses make money, their primary intention is to be of service. You engage this Vortex when you make an effort to support such establishments.

Conscious businesses are enterprises (both for- and not-for-profit) that strive to be aware of the effects of their actions, and be of conscious benefit to human and other living beings. Such enterprises are committed to "do no harm policy," take concrete steps to be aware of social and environmental impact of their activity — and act upon such awareness. They seek to promote happiness and systematically help their employees, shareholders, and clients to grow in awareness as conscious part of their business plan.

Today much of our money still flows toward enterprises that support this planet in talk but not in deed. Nowadays most companies peddle environmentally friendly messages because the public want to hear this. But talk is cheap! "Good thoughts are no better than good dreams, unless they be executed", said Ralph Waldo Emerson.

When you deal with conventional (i.e., unconscious) businesses their bad practices rub off on you. Limiting such exposure is a good idea if you wish to continue raising your vibration, which is the only fool-proof way for you to help the planet and its inhabitants.

Conscious business practices imply sustainable business practices but not the other way around. Don't confuse the current trend towards more sustainable business practices with conscious business. A sustainable business includes a strong service component — beyond mere sustainability.

You engage this Vortex when you vote with your wallet for awareness. Let your vote be in support for conscious businesses.

Action: Support, start, and engage conscious business establishments.

8.5 Engage locally

> Never doubt that a small group of thoughtful,
> committed citizens can change the world.
> Indeed, it's the only thing that ever has.
> — Margaret Mead

Locally is where your neighbors are. The closer you are to people the more potential is there to form real relationships. This Vortex is invoked when you realize that real engagement does not hide behind a veneer, digital or otherwise.

Local is where we invest our emotional, cultural, and social capital. Local is where we should invest our financial resources. Local is where we have a potential to grow roots. Local is where we build strong communities.

Yes, the Internet makes it easier to connect to people across the world, forming communities that are local in nature but dispersed geographically. Worldwide communication revolution of the Internet is a great innovation that allows us to communicate with our friends and colleague in faraway places. But engaging a real person sitting next to you is more substantial.

Yet, there is a tendency in the world today to buy and sell cheap, and not just the consumer goods (groceries, TVs, etc.). It cheapens everything else. Local is where it is hard to be cheap in spirit or in work, for your neighbors will notice and your reputation will suffer. As for consumer goods, nowadays cheap is defined by its sticker price, rather than the real cost of a product. Prices fall with cheap transportation cost (by ignoring eco-damage the future generations will have to deal with) and cheap labor (because poor foreign people are easily exploited, for they have limited choices). But at what hidden cost?

When manufacturing leaves your local community, the good jobs go as well. People suffer joblessness because they cannot or do not want to move, or are not educated, intelligent, or young enough to switch careers. Wouldn't it be better if everyone was employed with decent wages and could buy slightly more expensive locally manufactured TVs and groceries?

As a typical example, almost everything we buy today in the United States is manufactured in Asia. Not only this is unsustainable with regard to transportation costs and environmental damage that causes, it also disempowers people locally because their jobs are lost. (In the long-term, it does not help people in Asia either. Talk to anyone working in the call centers or in the factories that manufacture goods for the West and you will know how much they don't enjoy working there.)

What makes it possible for business to manufacture in one place and sell in another place? Cheap fuel for the moment is part of this. But more importantly, the rich have portable, liquid money. Money is an abstraction of economic energy. As a symbol or materialized metaphor, it is not real, like gold or wheat. Money allows you to work at one place but buy goods at another. It is a convenient way to exchange energy (barter) for mutual benefit. With money being an abstraction, why should you care if you invest in China or the US? Engaging locally is about keeping this energy flowing near you.

Global markets "connect" supply and demand with an abstract, ephemeral (non)reality of money. There cannot be good quality control for the supplier, the purchaser, and the goods. You get a mortgage, which is packaged with many other mortgages and sold to far away investors who do not care about you. Not much prevents the faraway bank's executive from foreclosing on your house in careless error, removing your possessions while you were out, and saying oops with no real recourse (all of which has actually happened many times). You don't care about them too because your relationship with them is not real — you will never meet the "oops" man in your own neighborhood. What will happen if people stop believing in the metaphor of money, just like they stopped believing in the institution of monarchy two hundred years ago?

Supporting local business is beneficial to society. Wouldn't you rather have a good job and pay a little more for the stuff you want than have lots of cheap goods and no job? Any time you buy imported goods that could be locally produced you are literally depriving your neighbors of work. Yes, international trade is good, but who is really benefitting? Rampant drive to make, sell, and buy cheaper has a very dangerous side effect — it transfers money away from people who are engaged in the production or use of the goods. If money loses its "realness" because of an economic disillusionment, it will not mean much to your local businesses. They will simply switch to barter in real goods.

Local production of goods is also a security and safety issue. As an example, let's look at food, which is a basic necessity. In USA, our food is primarily grown in California and Florida. We are amazingly efficient in agriculture. But what will happen if there is a problem with transportation due to a manmade or natural disaster? We also import food from China with ridiculously minimal controls for quality and safety.

Think globally, engage locally. We are one universal family and need to think for the welfare of the whole world. But when you engage locally you keep the social and financial energy flowing within the local community.

Action: Engage local people, communities, and businesses.

8.6 Collaborate!

> Walk as if you are kissing the earth with your feet.
> — Thich Nhat Hahn

There is great joy in working together. You engage this Vortex when you realize this.

Collaboration is about replacing the outdated, self-aggrandizing, profit motive with the love-inspired "we are all in this together" motive for doing anything in this world. Its inspiration comes from the fundamental recognition that we are not alone in the world. We live and share with others.

There is not intrinsic problem with the profit motive. But it does train you to focus on the short-term gratification and on the ego-aggrandizing that isolates, alienates, and leads away from happiness. That is why there are so many unhappy people in the countries where the profit motive is encouraged or culturally sanctioned.

At a deeper level, the world is moving towards win-win cooperative collaborative solutions. People are very tired of being alienated, lone individuals who think only of their tiny microcosm. Collaboration — out of love and desire to contribute — is the future. Don't let cynicism (yours or theirs) lead you to believe otherwise.

Recent increase in participation in open source projects is evidence and a good example of the things yet to come. An open source project is a collaborative creation, open for anyone to contribute to its evolution and free for anyone to use it. Open source is about working together out of love, where the process of creation matters more than results. People work on open source projects because they want to and can start or stop contributing any time they want to. It is the most natural way to work on any product or project. And when you have a lot of people who contribute, the quality of the offering radically increases.

Open source collaboration fosters transparency. Integrity of a project is naturally promoted when anyone can join in, participate, and observe. In an open collaboration, there is no pressure to hide mistakes. Errors are openly admitted. When a milestone is reached, everyone is invited for a celebration. Open collaboration is light, open, vibrant, and focused on good for all.

When you collaborate, you acknowledge your interconnectedness to the beings in this universe through your work environment. Interconnectedness is responsible for the saying "what goes around comes around". When you share, someone will share with you — one day or every day. Collaboration done well is a large deposit into your "spiritual virtue" account. Guess what such awareness will do to your bottom line as you focus on creating something good and new, while having faith in the "do what you love, money will follow" maxim?

Action: Participate in win-win cooperative solutions. Work together for fun and good!

9 Vortexes for Inspiring Life

I love that this morning's sunrise
does not define itself by last night's sunset.
— Steve Maraboli

The secret of success is constancy to purpose.
— Benjamin Disraeli

9.1 Action is king

> It is a thousand times more sensible
> to climb one foot up the mountainside
> than to chatter for years about the mountaintop.
> — Vernon Howard

> How beggarly appear arguments before a defiant deed.
> — Walt Whitman

> Do you want to know who you are? Don't ask. Act!
> Action will delineate and define you.
> — Witold Gombrowicz

You enter this Vortex when you realize that to truly know something direct experience is a must. Knowledge comes from a real engagement of a significant duration.

Human ego has an amazing capacity for imagination. It also has an incredible capacity to confuse imagination with reality — to distort perceiving with conceiving. We believe our imagination because we perceive experiences through our imagination. When we experience, our imagination receives and filters the information from the experience. When we believe our imagination, this imagination of ours is the source of information. This is similar to the difference between a documentary and an acted movie.

On the path to the Real, you move to where you must go by going there, not by studying a map, real or imagined. Engaging or confronting reality, internal or external, through action, internal or external, is the only way to go beyond the stronghold of imagination.

Human beings have powerful imagination. Our potent imagination defines us but it also presents us with the most challenge. In youth, we use our young and fresh mind to compensate for inexperience. We do it by imagining knowledge.

A smart youth can imitate knowledge very well, without being conscious of the pretense. Mature knowledge is attained only through action. Same is true for any endeavor, in which we are young beginners.

A spiritual system must focus on action to be authentic. Reading books or talking to friends feeds imagination but does not supply experience. An evolved spiritual aspirant, young or not, will intuitively know they don't know and engage with a system, such as these Vortexes. To quote Yoda, "There is no try, only do." The engagement will accelerate the accumulation of experience and will force quickening of the spiritual evolution of the aspirant.

Forced action solves the conflict of authenticities. One authenticity inside you may want one action, and another will want another action. The most common conflict is between what consensus reality (the groupthink of society) wants you to do and what your soul — your innermost self — calls you to do. You may face a choice between doing art and pursuing spirituality, or have a conflict between wanting a well-paying job and living in a monastery. Which direction to take? Only direct engaging will let you know — what you truly want will stick to you.

Real knowledge comes from experience. Experience comes from engagement. It does not come from reading books, listening to talks, or thinking about it. You have to put in time and effort to know something. However sophisticated it may be, daydreaming will not do.

Action: Only action leads to real knowledge. Don't talk, engage!

9.2 Perfection

He who wants to have right without wrong,
Order without disorder,
Does not understand the principles
Of heaven and earth.
— Chuang Tzu

Be ye perfect, even as your Father
which is in Heaven is Perfect.
— Jesus (Matthew 5:48).

Shantidasa said: "Life is perfect exactly the way it is; no one ever said perfection must be consistent." You enter this Vortex when you realize that perfection does not have to be consistent with your microcosmic desires.

You enter Vortex when you feel in your bones (know directly) that the world and you are perfect, with nothing to fix, nothing to change. This opens you up to real change, from a relaxed place and the position of strength.

This World and you — being a part of It — are creation of Cosmic Mind. You are a creation of this ever-evolving Universe, and you live your life as a part of this Universe. The process of change that you are going through at any given moment is the process the Universe is going through. To entertain different thoughts is to be out of tune with God's plan for you. To think differently is to doubt God. This Vortex is about doing your best to be in tune with this perfection.

You do not need to strive to be different, you do not need to change anything in your life. Everything is perfect, both pain and pleasure, night and day, black or white, green and yellow, young and old. It is all how it's supposed to be. So, relax and ignore the little voice in your head that wants you, someone, or something to be different — thinner, fatter, quieter, louder, smarter, older, greener.

The question then comes, "What is this spiritual path about, if there is nothing to change, nothing to do? The Path implies movement, doesn't it?" The path is about recognizing perfection, and while on your way to this recognition, recognizing that you do not always think so.

The Path can be compared to grass growing in easy or in harsh location. Grass can grow in a lush field, or it can grow through tough, inhospitable asphalt. In both cases, it is alive and moving forward. But each environment will lend different qualities to the grass. You might prefer to be in an open field, or you may prefer to be in an environment that calls for difficulties. A dry desert hill will make you strong, deep, and persistent. A lush, well-watered meadow will make you look beautiful and expect instant success, but the depth might not develop.

Grass grows where the seeds have been blown by the winds of life. And so do you, all your plans notwithstanding. There is a mysterious perfection that unfolds when you realize that you are not in control. God is in control. Things happen, and you may or may not like some of the happenings. But as you allow God's plan for you to unfold, you develop a higher vision — the knowing that everything is always perfect because Higher Intelligence knows what It is doing. In a way, this is about not taking yourself (your microcosmic position) too seriously. So, let God write the book of your life.

Focusing on perfection, rather than the imperfect is about focusing on the positive. Positive focus opens you up to possibilities, rather than closing you off to experience and joy. When you recognize that you are perfect the way you are, you open up to life — to being free.

Everyone has something to improve. But being dissatisfied with your current state and looking for improvements makes you imprisoned by your own attitude — your own idea of perfection, as something you achieve by applying effort. This breeds discontent about who you are and where you currently stand. Is this a good attitude with regard to where you want to go?

But if you tell yourself that you are good enough and everything in your life is moving as it should, and you will relax, expect being content, and a happy smile will begin lurking on your face.

Notions of imperfection are externally imposed. A cat knows she is perfect because she does not care about what others think of her. We humans care because we were conditioned to care as children. As our parents and society socialized us into the "world", they also socialized us away from our innate knowing of our perfection. Learn anew to love yourself, love your life, and to live in the moment, just as you knew how before "educators" educated you out of it. The Path is indeed about remembering who you are.

Action: Feel and cherish the perfection of the moment. Recognize that you and the world around you are as good as it gets.

9.3 Focus on positive action

> Wisdom is knowing what to do next.
> Virtue is doing it.
> — David Starr Jordan

You step into this Vortex when you focus on the positive action. Being positive is about looking forward. It is about directing your energy toward where you want to go, rather than spending your energy pondering over what has held you back in the past. Thus, this Vortex is about using your energy properly — for productive endeavors.

The teaching behind this Vortex was conceived as an effective tool for fighting bad habits. Working on developing positive habits is more effective than trying to eliminate bad habits — because what you resist persists!

What you resist tends to stay in your consciousness. If you focus on the positive action, then the positive will stay in your consciousness and will grow to dominate all aspects of your life. Your bad habits will simply begin to fall away due to inattention and disuse. It is always better to focus on doing what you truly want, rather than fighting against what you don't want.

Positive focus opens you up to new possibilities and better odds. Everyone has something to improve. But working on eliminating the bad implies being dissatisfied with your current state — it is about engaging your mind with the unwanted. This breeds discontent about who you are and where you stand. It is hard to achieve what you want if you run a thought-loop in your head, hating yourself and your circumstances.

Positive company helps with positive focus. Develop friends and colleagues who are better than you. Their company will constantly remind you of the direction toward which you want to go. Their influence will support you. Surrounding yourself with successful people helps soften the extremes in our spiritual and worldly life.

(Success is about the accomplishment of living a fulfilling and happy life. Being happy living in rags under a bridge is more successful that having it all in the world — a big house, beautiful wife, smart kids, cushy job, and a fat bank account — but being miserable inside. Being responsible to society is fine, but you should also be responsible to your spirit. Happiness is not a static state: what makes you happy now may not satisfy you in the future.)

Focusing on the positive action is about seeing the glass half-full, not half-empty. It is about being real and choosing the best action under the circumstances. It is about being an active optimist.

Action: Generate positive habits by focusing on positive actions.

9.4 Question beliefs

> There is only one cause of unhappiness:
> the false beliefs you have in your head,
> beliefs so widespread, so commonly held,
> that it never occurs to you to question them.
> — Anthony de Mello

This Vortex encourages you to look at your thought patterns and consider whether they are useful. You enter this Vortex any time you question certainty of your beliefs.

Beliefs are thoughts that you keep on thinking. Beliefs color your perception of reality. You see what you believe. Your beliefs cause you to ignore what is not in the inventory of your worldview. Your beliefs are, therefore, a self-fulfilling prophecy. On the path to freedom (i.e., your spiritual path), you need to crack the nut of your beliefs, however cherished, or you will fail in your spiritual endeavor. Freedom implies being free to make choices without being imprisoned by your thought habits.

Your beliefs construct the reality around you. Your beliefs bring things, events, and circumstances into your life — to present evidence for their "truth". For example, if you believe you are poor, you will tend toward poverty in your life. This is true for both financial and emotional deficits. If you believe that you are successful, you will attract money to yourself. If you believe that you are good at something, you will tend to become better at it.

Culture, religion, and family are sources of beliefs. Look in any place where humans live — a solitary cave, an urban home, an office, or a temple — and you will find beliefs. They might seem strange if they are not your own. Some people believe in freedom and democracy, even though they are full of irrational thoughts and want to impose such thinking on others. Some societies believe they are the most spiritual culture, even though they confuse spirituality with colorful religious thinking. A financially rich cultural empire takes as its prerogative to spread their ideas about human rights, happiness, progress, and freedom to all inhabitants of this world.

Religions are also collections of persistent thoughts, probably the most stuck belief systems human ever concocted. Religious and cultural beliefs are usually closely related and intertwined. Most religions believe their scripture to be the best source of information, even though it was written by people hundreds of years ago and there are many other holy books with similar claims on truth and God. Just like the schizophrenic *Three Christs of Ypsilanti*, most religious people tacitly consider other religions delusional. "I am right, others are wrong — overwhelming evidence to the contrary notwithstanding!" The belief that a higher power or a "sacred" text demands compliance to a belief is also a belief.

Family "wisdom" passed down the generations is another source of beliefs that need to be examined critically. For example, families frequently dictate how many children one must have, the dress one must wear, the profession one must choose, the religion one must follow, etc. Enter the black cat that crosses your way and curses your day. Poor black cat!

Not all beliefs are bad. Beliefs allow a group of people who share a common origin or purpose to communicate with each other without the need to constantly explain every detail. Words and grammar of human (and machine) languages are a useful collection of beliefs, for example. The association of sound patterns (spoken words) with objects, thoughts, feelings, or events they name is a belief system. Professionals have beliefs that derive from scientific basis of their trade. Many cultures pass important knowledge by word of mouth down the generations.

We humans, however, have a tendency not to examine our beliefs. In part, this tendency is due to the blindfold mask any belief system naturally introduces. We must learn to break out of these thought-prisons. We must examine all beliefs carefully because they control how we perceive — they introduce bias to how we see the world.

Thus, you need to examine carefully whether any of your thoughts are worth thinking. The questions you should ask are: "Is this thought useful to me and my world? Is this belief serving my higher good and that of others?"

Here is a very incomplete list of common beliefs in Western culture (and beyond) to take a look at:

- I am going to live until the age X. I have Y number of years to enjoy life, work, care for my children, retire, etc. You do not know how long you have left.

- I have to work hard and long for my life to be successful. Successful people work well, not hard.

- You are immoral if you do not believe in God. Human beings — if not dysfunctional — are innately moral.

- You must believe in God to be spiritual. Authentic spirituality has nothing to do with a belief in God. It is about direct experience, a real transformation.

Reality is vast. It is far greater and complex than our beliefs about It allow. Our fragile ego protects itself from this Immensity by letting in only the information it considers useful — and filtering out the rest. These filters are beliefs, and they constitute the very nature of ego. Beliefs provide a sense of security and stability in the face of wild, raw, and unfathomable Reality out there. Beliefs make human life in society possible and palatable.

We should always remember that beliefs are tool for better living. They are not the end in themselves. Throw out the beliefs that do not work.

Action: Examine your beliefs; let go of the ones that do not serve you.

9.5 Be here now!

> Dream as if you'll live forever,
> live as if you'll die today.
> — James Dean

> Happiness is to be found along the way,
> not at the end of the road,
> for then the journey is over and it is too late.
> Today, this hour, this minute is
> the day, the hour, the minute for each of us
> to sense the fact that life is good,
> with all of its trials and troubles,
> and perhaps more interesting because of them.
> — Robert R. Updegraff

Present moment is all there is! You engage this Vortex when you realize that the NOW is the narrow gap through which you enter and live your life.

The present moment is the time when you experience, when you feel yourself alive, when you enjoy. Everything else is a mental game that the mind likes to play. Why carry the past with you? The past does not determine the future — what you do now does! Why worry about the future? You do not know what might happen ten minutes from now. Focus on the NOW where your life happens.

Yet, we rarely focus on the present. Our brain uses past experiences as a reference to scheme about the future. This is our mind's nature. However, the past is just a memory thought wave you experience in the present. You can't be sure if the past has happened or not. Corroboration by the fellow humans can be dismissed via the "consensus reality" argument. You have no way of knowing if the past has actually happened or is imagined by all the humans collectively. The only thing you do know is that you remember your past. Similarly, the future is also but a thought in the present moment.

In essence, entering this Vortex is about cultivating the beginner's mind. Beginner's mind doesn't worry about what happened in the past. It is not heavy with past experiences that interfere with the new ones. Mind of a beginner is fresh and open to experience. Beginner's mind does not know — it is ready to learn the new. Beginner's mind is naturally relaxed, happy, and working for something good. It is focused on the NOW.

Not properly planning for the future stems from a confusion of spiritual and mundane worlds. A responsible person knows the difference. He or she plans calmly and deliberately, without being overly concerned about the past, without fear and worry, without becoming overwhelmed — in the NOW.

Focusing on the present moment is about the difference between thriving and surviving. To fully live your life you must savor the NOW.

Action: The present moment is all you've got. Use it — be it!

Final Thoughts

There comes a time in a man's life
when to get where he has to go —
if there are not doors or windows —
he walks through a wall.
— Bernard Malamud

If you're interested in something, you do what's convenient.
If you're committed to something, you do whatever it takes.
— John Assaraf

There is no greater gift you can give or receive than
to honor your calling. It's why you were born.
And how you become most truly alive.
— Oprah Winfrey

What's next?

The minute I heard my first love story,
I started looking for you, not knowing
how blind that was.
Lovers don't finally meet somewhere.
They're in each other all along.
— Jalaluddin Rumi

A ship in harbor is safe,
but that is not what ships are built for.
— John Augustus Shedd

The way to wisdom is through action. All you need to start is a human body, reasonable intelligence, an open mind that is curious to learn — and a real desire. Talking about it, reading books about it, or studying a scripture do not substitute asking real questions that are necessary to receive real answers.

Real questions come from real engagements that really change your perspective. It is the change in perspective that summons new ideas and solutions.

Start with Phase I: Taste the experience. Focus on the four Universal Vortexes; they are universal for a reason. When positive results begin to trickle in — usually within a month or two — make sure you acknowledge your achievement in your mind and hold a small celebration with friends — so that your success is registered in your memory.

Engaging the Vortexes is free. Classes, coaching and mentoring, and retreats are reasonably priced — teacher and the organization that supports the teaching have to pay the bills. If you can't afford an event, contact us and we will do our best to work with you. We want people who are ready and eager to benefit from our teachings!

Action: Don't wait. Engage NOW!

Acknowledgements

I wish to pay my homage to all the remarkable teachers that came on my way. Their contribution reverberates in the Cosmos and in my mind. I sincerely hope that what I am passing on is worthy of their teachings to me.

I wish to offer heart-felt thanks to Mike Kremen for numerous insightful comments as well as editing and proofreading. Mike's reliable participation and commitment made this book possible. I also wish to thank Joshua Duke and Randy Goldberg for many useful comments and suggestions and Jamie Chandler and Diane Bongiorni for proofreading some of the text.

I have written this book based on my experience and have relied on my memory. There is a good chance, however, that I might have used concepts that were not invented by me. In particular, I want to acknowledge Eckhart Tolle for the excellent new term "Pain body", which is a better name for a particular type of the mind-ego-personality distortion than karma or samskara, a known concept for at least two thousand years.

I also wish to acknowledge Esther Hicks and her Law of Attraction work for the inspiration behind the Vortexes that talk about intentionality and encourage conscious focus on discovering our true desires. (These Vortexes are "Day intending", "Period intending", and "Madhuvidya".) I also wish to thank her for inspiring the term "Vortex" itself, which I use with a completely different meaning. Esther Hicks uses it to describe the state of "being in the zone", while I use the term to describe a discrete teaching that draws you in, rather than instructing.

I also would like to thank the folks at Wikipedia, the free encyclopedia, which I have consulted online for an occasional definition.

About the author

Dr. Anatole has always been interested in helping people find meaning, purpose, passion, and joy in their lives. What always distinguished his work, however, is his steadfast focus on clarity, depth, competency, and real results. Dr. Anatole knows that each person's growth and evolution is a forward journey along a spiral ever reaching further.

Coming from a family of distinguished musicians, engineers, and architects, Anatole did not approach his own quest lightly. From the tender age of twelve, he doggedly pursued results that were real and deep. Early on, he understood that talk of food does not remove hunger; one must actually eat food, preferably of the nourishing, tasty, and colorful variety.

He was always skeptical about the standard narrative of birth, school, job, marriage, and kids, followed by death. Seeking freedom from this groupthink-endorsed trajectory, Dr. Anatole's work always focused on his peers, on people who are not inspired by the McLife.

On his quest for spiritual depth, Dr. Anatole risked everything. Facing inevitable spiritual upheavals and emotional tribulations, he had to stumble over his own mistakes and then correct them by himself. Due to this, understanding what skilled support is and then offering it has always been a priority for him.

For being unconventional, he encountered substantial personal, social, and financial pushback. Working through external obstacles and his own internal resistance, Anatole achieved a vision of transrational truth and reality that he is now putting into words, to understand his own journey and more importantly be of worthy help to others.

Resources

www.modernseers.org

contact@modernseers.org

Reader reviews

Word of mouth is essential for an author like myself to get noticed. If you enjoyed this book, please consider writing a short review wherever you purchased it or on Goodreads. Also, consider if any friends would enjoy it. I would very much appreciate it!

Support the author

I rely on kindness of people like you to pay my bills. If you found this book helpful or enjoyable, please consider supporting my work on Patreon or PayPal.

https://www.patreon.com/anatole
https://www.paypal.me/anatole

If you wish to make a tax-deductible donation, please use:
https://www.paypal.me/modernseers
or use PayPal email: donations@modernseers.org

Modern Seers Inc. is registered as a California Nonprofit Corporation and has been recognized on the federal level by the IRS as a 501(c)(3) charity since 1994.

No solicitations please!

www.ingramcontent.com/pod-product-compliance
Lightning Source LLC
LaVergne TN
LVHW092323080426
835508LV00039B/517